Published for
**OXFORD INTERNATIONAL
AQA EXAMINATIONS**

International
INDEPENDENT PROJECT QUALIFICATION

Mary James

OXFORD
UNIVERSITY PRESS

Great Clarendon Street, Oxford, OX2 6DP, United Kingdom

Oxford University Press is a department of the University of Oxford. It furthers the University's objective of excellence in research, scholarship, and education by publishing worldwide. Oxford is a registered trade mark of Oxford University Press in the UK and in certain other countries

© Oxford University Press 2018

The moral rights of the authors have been asserted

First published in 2018

All rights reserved. No part of this publication may be reproduced, stored in a retrieval system, or transmitted, in any form or by any means, without the prior permission in writing of Oxford University Press, or as expressly permitted by law, by licence or under terms agreed with the appropriate reprographics rights organization. Enquiries concerning reproduction outside the scope of the above should be sent to the Rights Department, Oxford University Press, at the address above.

You must not circulate this work in any other form and you must impose this same condition on any acquirer

British Library Cataloguing in Publication Data
Data available

978-019-842608-0

10 9 8 7 6

Paper used in the production of this book is a natural, recyclable product made from wood grown in sustainable forests. The manufacturing process conforms to the environmental regulations of the country of origin.

Printed and bound by CPI Group (UK) Ltd, Croydon, CR0 4YY

This book draws on an earlier work, *Extended Project Student Companion*, which was published in association with Gatsby Technical Education Projects and the Nuffield Foundation Curriculum Programme. The author and publisher thank those organizations for their assistance on the earlier publication. Links to third party websites are provided by Oxford in good faith and for information only. Oxford disclaims any responsibility for the materials contained in any third party website referenced in this work.

Please note that the Practice Questions in this book allow students a genuine attempt at practising exam skills, but they are not intended to replicate examination papers.

Cover image: David Mala/Getty Images.
Artwork by: Q2A Media Pvt. Ltd.

Table of contents

Introduction 5
    What is the IPQ, and how does it fit into my studies? 5
    The process involved in an IPQ 7
    How will my Independent Project be assessed? 12
    Checklist: are you ready to start your Independent Project? 14

1 Project management skills: starting out 15
    Choosing a topic 16
    Building up an initial project idea 22
    From 'working' title to final title 23
    Working independently 24
    Checklist: are you ready for your initial ideas review
    meeting with your supervisor? 25
    Initial planning for your project 27
    Project planning techniques 30
    Drawing up a detailed project plan 31
    Organisational skills – keeping your project on track 32
    Project proposal and approval 34
    Checklist: are you ready for your planning review meeting? 35

2 Project management skills: researching the project 37
    Taught element 37
    Project management 38
    What sort of skills will I need to develop? 39
    Oxford AQA assessment objectives 40
    The grading process 42
    Research methods 43
    Identifying likely resources 44
    Evaluating your resources 45
    Using the Internet effectively as a research tool 49
    Using people as subjects in your research 51
    Reading strategies to help you gather relevant
    information quickly 55
    Representing information in your own way 57
    Using ICT to support your research 59
    Risk assessment 62
    Skills to help your project run smoothly 64
    Statistics: strengths and weaknesses 66

Decision making and problem solving skills 68
Creative thinking 71
Your mid-term review 73
Examples of students' work 76
Planning your project product (written report) 78
Checklist – are you ready for your mid-term review? 79

3 Project management skills: producing the project product 81
Report writing skills 82
Using visuals in your report 85
Think about the language of your report 88
Manage the writing process 89
Structuring your report 90
Avoid plagiarism 93
Referencing your sources 95
Oxford AQA Exams IPQ Assessment Objectives 99
List of required material for grading 101
*Checklist – are you ready for your project
product review meeting?* 102

4 Presenting your project 104
Different presentation styles: what should your
presentation consist of? 105
Presentation skills 108
Communicating clearly 110
*Checklist – are you ready for your presentation
and question and answer session?* 116

5 Finalising and submitting your project 119
Evaluation and reflection 120
Completing your Project Production Log 122
Checklist – are you ready for your project submission? 124

Introduction

By the end of this section, you should:
- ✔ have a good idea of what the International Independent Project Qualification (IPQ) is
- ✔ identify how you might benefit from and enjoy the IPQ
- ✔ understand what might be expected of you in your Independent Project.

What is the IPQ, and how does it fit into my studies?

The IPQ is an opportunity to do a project in a subject area which interests you. It will help you develop critical thinking and project management skills which will help in other studies, either now or if you move on to university or a professional career. The IPQ assesses your ability to plan, carry out, report on, and evaluate an independent **project**.

The emphasis of the assessment is on the entire **planning and** research process, a presentation and report, and **other** appropriate evidence of your work. It is a level 3 qualification which may be followed alongside **your** (international) A levels.

The IPQ assesses your ability to plan, carry out, report on, and evaluate a project.

IPQ as a free-standing qualification

Your Independent Project is an extension to your GCSE AS/A levels, or any other academic qualification you are following in school. You can choose an area of study related to your AS/A-levels, but the two must not overlap. You could also choose a very different area of study from your main subject areas.

Although the IPQ is an entirely free-standing qualification for which you are awarded a grade (just like your AS/A-levels), research has shown that completing a research project like this can help you achieve a higher grade in your A-levels. Research by the Centre for Education Research and Practice in the UK showed that students taking a very similar project-based qualification are 29% more likely to achieve a Grade A*-B in most of their standard A-level subjects. So whilst the IPQ is quite separate to your A-level subjects, it will help you develop skills which will also benefit your other studies.

How is the IPQ different from my other studies?

There are five key elements which make the IPQ special.
- It requires independent research and learning to extend your studies.
- You must choose your topic and project title in negotiation with your Supervisor.
- You have to show that you can plan, deliver and present your project work.
- There is some teaching of necessary skills involved, but the majority of your learning will require your own self motivation and organisational skills.
- Your work will be monitored and 'mentored' by a Project Supervisor; they may suggest other people who can also help you.

How will the Independent Project be of benefit to me?

The Independent Project should be enjoyable and fulfilling. It will also be challenging, so you need to have a clear idea of why you want to do the qualification and how it could benefit you.

- Completing the Independent Project will help you develop your own organisational, project management and independent learning skills. These skills will help you become a more confident student in other areas of study.
- The skills you develop as part of the Independent Project will provide you with a good foundation in study and research skills. These skills will help you in your university studies, if you choose to go on to higher education, and at work.
- Successfully completing the Independent Project Qualification is also likely to enhance your application to higher education. If you apply to a UK university, the IPQ will be recognised as equivalent to half an A level. It will help you to stand out from other students, both in your personal statement and at interview – this is particularly important when applying for popular university courses such as medicine and law, or if you are making an application to a top university in the US or anywhere else in the world.
- Because you are following an area of personal interest, the project will bring freshness to your studies, and might help you decide on a future career or what you will study at university.

The process involved in an IPQ

What will I be required to do?

The Oxford International AQA Examinations Independent Project Qualification[1] has been independently validated by the UK examinations regulator Ofqual. It has specific requirements.

You will have to do the following:

1. Choose your topic or your area of interest and develop a title that will form your individual project and submit this for formal approval.
2. Identify and draft the main aims and objectives of your project. Aims are broad, general statements about what you hope your project will achieve. Objectives are specific statements about what your project will cover. The objectives should contain action verbs such as 'identify', 'contrast', 'analyse', and 'construct'.
3. Plan, research and carry out your project. This will mean that you have to apply certain organisational skills and strategies to fulfil your objectives. You will also have to obtain and select information from a number of different sources, analyse your data and show that you understand the complexities of the topic you've chosen.
4. Document and evaluate all stages of your project process. There are certain essential requirements: you will, for example, have to complete a Production Log.
5. Produce a written report of 5000 words.
6. Prepare and give a ten-minute live presentation about your project and the process. You will need to present your project in a way that is appropriate for a non-specialist audience: this will be in a form that is appropriate for your chosen topic. This will be followed by a ten-minute live question and answer session.

---

[1] © Oxford International AQA Exams Please refer to the current version of the specification on the Oxford AQA Exams website at www.oxfordaqaexams.org.uk/subjects/projects/ipq

Introduction

7. Review and reflect on the whole project process. This includes assessing if your project fulfils the original aims, as well as reflecting on your own learning during the process of producing your project.

You won't be doing this entirely on your own. You will have the help and support of a Project Supervisor in your school – probably a teacher you know already, or another member of staff. Some students may also discuss their project with a Specialist Consultant and meet with them to discuss progress. If you feel like you would like to work with a Specialist Consultant, discuss this with your Project Supervisor. You should also check the exact requirements of the project with a current version of the IPQ specification.

Material required for assessment

You must submit the following as evidence for assessment:
- the completed Production Log and Assessment Record, including the Project Proposal Form, Presentation Record (and a recording of your presentation), and the Candidate Record Form
- your written report and relevant appendices, depending on the topic or subject you choose.

Will there be any lessons?

Completing the Independent Project Qualification will be more about learning for yourself than being taught by your teacher. After all, you need to develop your independent research and learning skills. However there is a taught element, and your teachers will be able to give you more information on the form this will take in your school.

Although you and your peers will be doing very different topics, there will be some skills you can learn and develop as a group.

Here are some examples:
- There are accepted forms for academic writing which may be useful to you in structuring your written work. This will be important when you come to write up your report.
- Project management skills are needed, including how you manage your work within the time available, how you manage the resources you have access to, and how to search effectively for relevant information using libraries, the internet and other sources.
- How to carry out your project safely and effectively. If you are carrying out some practical work, for example, in a science laboratory, you will need to know about laboratory health and safety. For other types of research involving members of the public you may need to adhere to certain professional codes of conduct. (All students must carry out a full risk assessment prior to starting their project.

How will I work with my Supervisor?

Although there is a strong element of you working independently and taking responsibility for your own research, this does not mean there will be no support on offer for you.

At your school or college, there will be a teacher or a member of staff who will be appointed as your Supervisor. Your Supervisor will support you along the journey from project proposal through to submission.

> **Key term**
>
> **Submission** The formal word that awarding bodies use to refer to 'giving in' or 'handing in' work or material to be assessed.

> **Study tip**
>
> Remember that the Assessment Objectives focus on the process involved in your project, the evidence and your written report, as well as how you evaluate your own learning throughout that process.

> **Key term**
>
> **Assessment Objectives** The AOs are a set of criteria published by Oxford AQA exams which you are required to meet. Your work will be compared to these AOs when your work is being graded.
>
> **Specialist Consultant** You may choose to seek the advice of someone who is an expert (or who 'specialises') in your subject area to discuss your project ideas or progress. This person won't assess your work, nor make any decisions for you. Discuss with your Project Supervisor if you think a person like this could be helpful for you.

Working with your Supervisor

At the very beginning of your project process, it would be useful for you to establish answers to the following questions with your Supervisor.

- How will you communicate? By email? Face-to-face? By phone?
- How often will you meet?
- Will you be able to contact your Supervisor during school/college holidays?
- If your Supervisor is not available, who should you discuss things with?
- How should you prepare for your face-to-face meetings?

Your Supervisor will be able to advise you on managing and developing your project but you will make your own decisions. You can choose not to take the advice. Remember, your presentation at the end of your project has to be aimed at a non-specialist audience. Your Supervisor may or may not be a subject specialist in your area of research. Discuss with your Supervisor if you would like to have the support of a Specialist Consultant.

Supervisor's responsibilities

The Supervisor's responsibilities will be, in broad terms, as shown in the table. Their main role is to guide you. You are responsible for owning your log and recording advice.

Project stage (Page numbers relate to the relevant sections in this book.)	What your Supervisor will do	What AQA requires the Supervisor to do
Starting out on your project see page 15	Meet with you to review your initial ideas and discuss how you intend to develop your initial idea into a full project Agree your working title and project proposal with you	Complete **Part B of the Candidate Record Form, Production Log and Assessment Record**, giving comments on your proposal
Researching your project see page 37	Post proposal acceptance, meet with you to review your project plan Meet with you during your project to discuss progress	Conduct a mid-term review with you
Producing your written report see page 81	Meet with you to discuss the project as it nears its end	Conduct an end-of-project review with you
Presenting your project see page 104	Your Supervisor will be present at your presentation; you will be asked questions relating to your project and the presentation	Your Supervisor will record and comment on the delivery of your project
Finalising and submitting your project see page 119		Your Supervisor must endorse your **Candidate Record form, Production Log and Assessment Record and sign the front page**
Assessing your project		The completed Candidate Record Form, Production Log and Assessment Record, your written report (and any relevant appendices) a copy of your presentation are all provided as evidence for assessment. Supervisors give your work a grade, and confirm that all work is your own.

Can I work as part of a group?

The work for your project is intended to represent your own work as an individual. In line with this, Oxford AQA Exams do not allow work that is carried out as a group to be submitted for the international Independent Project.

> **Key term**
>
> **Appendices (plural for appendix)** are the additional material you may need to include with your report like a bibliography or list of references.

You may, of course, have lessons as a class or in a group where you are taught some skills to help you carry out your project.

What others might do to support you?

Librarians, in your school or college library or local public library, could help you with your research, by advising you on the availability of resources. You will be assessed on how well you obtain and select information from a variety of sources, so it's important that you explore all relevant options.

There may be other people whose skills and experience you can draw on and who may be very keen to help:
- your parents/guardians
- local employers or local businesses
- local universities
- local museums, galleries, theatres and other community organisations
- professional organisations and societies
- a Specialist Consultant, for example, members of staff within your school or college who have interests or recent research experience in your topic area.

You don't have to feel that independent learning is working alone. There are plenty of people who can advise and support you, and above all, you can always talk to your Supervisor.

Using this book

This book gives guidance on the journey you make whilst identifying, researching, and presenting your project and during the report writing phase. It is full of tips and techniques to help you develop and practise the skills required to carry out your project work successfully.
- This book introduces you to the skills required during each stage of your project, and explains how they will be important to your project work.
- It provides brief activities to help you learn, practise and apply the relevant skill.
- 'What this means to my project' helps you apply this learning to your individual project.
- 'Study Tips' help you understand the assessment process and how your project will be graded.
- 'Key Terms' highlight and explain important words or phrases.
- 'Checklists' help prepare you for meetings with your project Supervisor.
- 'Project Progress Checkpoints' highlight exactly what stage you are at in your project, and how it fits into the whole process. These will prompt you to make sure you are ready for the next stage of your project process.

This information on skills will be useful to any student doing an Independent Project. Your Supervisor may also give you additional activities to help you develop skills which may be specific to the subject area of your Independent Project.

How will my Independent Project be assessed?

See the table on the next pages.

What Oxford AQA Exams require?

Always check the most recent version of the specifications, as changes are made from time to time. The evidence for assessment you need to provide is:

1 The completed Production Log

Every student registered for this qualification has an Oxford AQA Exams Production Log. It provides the exam board with a documented record of the planning and progress of your project. It is your responsibility to make sure that every element is completed sequentially and at the appropriate time. You are not allowed to go back and complete this log retrospectively. (Your school may be using an electronic monitoring system like Project Q which doesn't allow this, anyway. Ask your teacher if you are in any doubt.) Each student also gives in a signed Candidate Record Form and Assessment Record.

2 A written report

All students must provide a written report and any relevant appendices. Your report should be 5000 words in length. You are allowed to write within +/− 10% of this which means your report should amount to more than 4500 words but less than 5500 words.

3 A record of your presentation

You have to provide a live 10-minute presentation to a non-specialist audience, followed by a 10-minute question and answer session. The presentation may include flipcharts, posters, Prezi, PowerPoint, or short video extracts. It's your choice. You must decide what medium suits your subject area and your audience. Make your decision in consultation with your Project Supervisor; your school may need you to fit in with other students' presentations, too.

Your assessment evidence must include a record of the live presentation. Your Supervisor will also provide a record of relevant questions you were asked and how you answered them.

Remember that your presentation must include reference to the whole project process, not just your research conclusions.

For the IPQ, the presentation can be carried out in your native language (ie it doesn't have to be in English, although your school might decide that this is a better option for you). If it is not in English, evidence needs to be provided in English for external moderation purposes.

How will my Independent Project be assessed?

Project stage (Page numbers relate to the relevant sections in this book.)	What you will do	What Oxford AQA Exams requires you to do
Starting out on your project see page 15	Select your topic/area of interest Draft a suggested title, aims, and objectives - this will be approved by your school/Supervisor Carry out a risk assessment to understand how to carry out every aspect of your research safely and to put measures in place to reduce any risks Carry out some initial research so that you can sufficiently develop your project aims and objectives and finalise your project title and research plan Agree the working title with your Supervisor	Complete the Record of initial ideas section of the Candidate Record Form, Production Log and Assessment Record Complete Part A: Candidate Proposal section of the Candidate Record Form, Production Log and Assessment Record [title of this form(s) tbc] Write a risk assessment
Researching your project see page 37	Conduct the research that your project plan requires to meet the aims and objectives you set yourself Record your research and the resources that you make use of Meet with your Supervisor regularly to discuss the project process and any issues you face. Record any action you take as a result of their advice or guidance. Record any changes you make to your plan and why you have decided to make these changes Finalise your project title, aims and objectives	Record your planning and research in the Candidate Record Form, Production Log and Assessment Record
Producing your project product see page 81	Produce your written report with relevant appendices	All students must provide a **written report** of 5000 words. Your appendices should include a full bibliography and any relevant references for your written report Complete the Project product review section of the Candidate Record Form, Production Log and Assessment Record
Presenting your project see page 104	Communicate findings from your project research and a review of the project process in a ten-minute live presentation Be prepared to answer questions about your project in a ten-minute session after this presentation	Deliver your presentation, targeted at a non-specialist audience and answer the questions you are asked Your presentation needs to be recorded in the **Production Log**, and your Supervisor will also complete the Production Log to confirm that your live presentation took place and provide evidence of the questions you were asked and how you answered them
Reviewing, finalising and submitting your project see page 119	Reflect on the process of planning, researching, writing up, and presenting your project	Complete your the Summary and reflection section of the Candidate Record Form, Production Log and Assessment Record, ensuring that it includes your reflections on the process of your project

Checklist: are you ready to start your Independent Project?

Your Independent Project should be a very rewarding and exciting educational experience. You will be expected to work independently and develop new skills, but you will have plenty of support through your project Supervisor and by using this resource.

Before starting on your Independent Project, make sure you are appropriately prepared for what it will involve. Make notes on the following[2].

	My response
The benefits to me of carrying out an Independent Project are …	
The implications of committing my time and resource to the Independent Project are …	
The following teachers are happy to provide me with appropriate support …	
I think that a topic for a good Independent Project could be …	
I will ensure that my Independent Project has an equal focus on both the project content and its process by …	
The time I have available to research my project and complete it appropriately is …	
The aspects of my project research which might incur some risk either to myself or the safety of others are … (eg using equipment safely)	
What else do I need to do? (such as people to talk to, and research on possible topics)	

▶▶▶ **Next steps**

You will be required to identify a suitable topic for your project and to explore the possible aims and objectives. See the next chapter of this book.

▶▶▶

---

[2]Filling in this chart is not an assessment requirement for your IPQ. However it may help you to prepare for an initial meeting with your Supervisor to agree your project ideas.

Project management skills: starting out

1

Getting started on your Independent Project will be an exciting time, allowing you some real independence in a chosen topic area that is likely to motivate and inspire you. Don't let that enthusiasm to 'get into it' stop you from taking time and effort to carefully plan your project research and identify your ultimate goals. It will help you succeed if you establish the aims and objectives for your project at the start, and make sure your project plan makes appropriate use of both time and available resources.

This chapter will help you to:

- ✔ think about what might influence your choice of topic for your Independent Project
- ✔ practise some techniques to help you identify some possible projects
- ✔ establish your project aims and objectives
- ✔ plan your project and explore the issues that will help you achieve your goals
- ✔ fulfil the requirements of Oxford AQA Exams' project approval process.

Your supervisor will support you

1 Project management skills: starting out

Choosing a topic

By the end of this section, you should be able to:
- ✔ explore the factors which might affect your choice of topic
- ✔ understand what we mean by 'independent' and how that will help you make your topic choice
- ✔ identify your suggested project aims and objectives
- ✔ understand the difference between a 'working' title and the 'final' title of your research project
- ✔ prepare for your initial planning meeting with your Project Supervisor to agree your project ideas.

What do we mean by 'independent'?

The 'independent' nature of the IPQ is what makes it unique at this level. It is that which sets it apart from anything you are likely to have done before in your studies. You have to make sure that your project matches this expectation for you to work entirely independently.

- It is a single and original piece of work carried out by you.
- It requires good quality planning and preparation by you.
- It requires you to use a high degree of independence in your research finding your own sources of material, taking notes, without copying directly without acknowledgement.
- It allows you to go beyond a single exam specification or subject area.
- It is a piece of work that doesn't duplicate something you are already doing as part of another qualification (eg in one of your A-levels), or that you have already submitted as part of an exam in the past.

It is a piece of work you do yourself, not as part of a group or with the input of others in your class. This means that you will be developing and extending a specific area of your studies, or a personal interest or activity, in such a way that your final project topic would not normally fall within your main programme of study.

So what does this mean in practice?
- You can't resubmit a piece of work that you have already completed as part of another examination.
- You can't reuse a project that you had already completed as part of another course of study.
- The topic for your project will not overlap with anything you are already studying. If you are studying History, you can do a historical topic, but it should, for example, be taken from a different time period to any which forms part of your A level studies.
- You work alone, but you are given plenty of support by teachers and/or your Project Supervisor (some students may also request the help of a Subject Specialist).

An Independent Project encourages real creativity, independent exploration, innovation, and to some extent, risk-taking. These will extend your own knowledge, skills and experience and underpin your development as a researcher.

Bear in mind this quotation from the eminent scientist, Albert Einstein, who developed the theory of relativity:

> 'If we knew what we were doing it wouldn't be research, would it?'

What does this mean in terms of level?

In terms of the level required, an Independent Project Qualification is a level 3 qualification, equivalent to A level standard. You may be doing it alongside AS levels or in year 12 (the first year of your A level studies), so have not necessarily reached an A level standard in other subject areas yet. To achieve this qualification, your work must reach the same level as an A level.

We've talked about the IPQ being the equivalent of an AS level. To be clear about this:
- The planning, research, execution, development of thinking, review, and presentation of your project must reflect an A level standard (so could be awarded an A*).
- The qualification is worth half an A level for university admission (UK).

When choosing the topic area for your research, it might be difficult to decide where to begin. Consider the questions on the next page – these might help lead you to your chosen area.

> **Key term**
>
> **Independent** Your project must be planned, researched, and carried out by you. Whilst you will have the support of your Supervisor, you have to make sure that your work is original and completed by you alone.
>
> **Dual accreditation** Your project topic must not overlap with any of your other studies. You cannot enter a piece of work for one assessment/accreditation and also submit it for your IPQ. That would represent dual accreditation and is not allowed.

Take a good hard look at yourself

> **ACTIVITY Look at yourself**
>
> **1** Think carefully about the following questions. These should prompt some thinking around topic areas that would reflect your skills, experience and personal interests.
>
>   **A** Which subject areas have you enjoyed?
>   (This might not be the same as those areas you know you are good at.)
>
>   **B** Which activities do you describe yourself as passionate about? (This might be an activity you do as part of your school life, or might be a hobby you do outside of school.)
>
>   **C** Of the following skills, which ones would you mark yourself with 7/10 or more?
>   - reading for an overview of text, and critically evaluating what you read
>   - putting people at ease and getting them to talk
>   - reading literary texts
>   - analysing information
>   - solving problems with an IT solution
>   - exploring the world around you
>   - reviewing multimedia and films
>
>   **D** Is there a topic or subject area you have always wanted to find out more about?
>
>   **E** What are you thinking of doing after school? Is there a topic that links with this? If you are going on to university to study, is there a topic which would really show your enthusiasm for the subject you have chosen to study?
>
>   **F** When you first thought about doing an IPQ, what was your first thought as to a suitable project? Gut instinct is often right! If there is an idea that keeps nagging away at you, go back to it.

Enjoy it!

Whatever you decide to do, and whatever research question you come up with, make sure it really interests you! You want to make sure you enjoy it! The IPQ, like most worthwhile ventures, is hard work, so you might be more successful if you are motivated by a project you can get passionate about.

What constraints might affect your topic choice?

Doing something you enjoy might provide lots of positive thinking and optimism, but you'll still need to keep your feet on the ground. Several factors might restrict your project choice.

> **ACTIVITY Constraints**
>
> **1** Consider the following questions. These may reveal some obstacles to your choice of topic area. You may want to make some notes, and discuss your answers with your Project Supervisor.
>
> **A** Does your project complement your other subject areas? Will it be easy to manage around your other subject commitments?
>
> **B** Have you been told that you can or can't make use of specialist accommodation or equipment? Do you need access to a science laboratory? Do you need certain chemicals? Will you or your school be able to obtain these?
>
> **C** Are there any cultural or religious customs which might affect what you choose to research or which prevent you from researching certain topic areas?
>
> **D** Are you or your school able to provide online access to the resources you might need? Is there a subscription to pay - how affordable is this?
>
> **E** Will you research resources in your native language? Or in English? Are all the resources you need to access available in the language you would like to use? Is there any vocabulary it would be useful for you to clarify before you start in the subject area you choose?

Study tip Above all, it's important to be motivated to learn about your chosen topic. This is one of the few study opportunities where you get to choose what you study - so choose well! Your Supervisor will help you.

Be inspired! – getting ideas to flow

People can be inspired in different ways. Some learners work hard whilst others sit back and seemingly wait for an idea to hit them. There are several techniques you can use to build up some original ideas for a project topic. You might use a spidergram to help generate some ideas. Ideas will come more easily once you start paying attention to them and start to nurture them.

Building up a spidergram

Start with a theme and write that down in the middle of a piece of paper. Relax, be open to ideas and just write down whatever that theme suggests to you. Don't reject anything you think of – note each point down as it occurs to you and allow it to connect in some way to the next. There are no right or wrong ideas – you just need to write something down and then let your mind think of the next idea. You could then circle the most relevant themes and create a new spidergram from each of those.

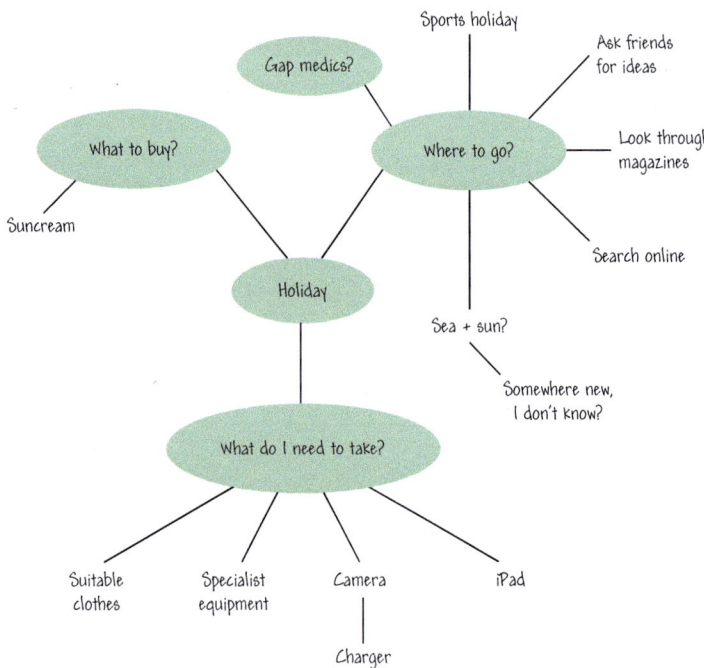

Change your perspective

As we grow up in a certain environment and culture, we tend to develop our own perspective that is personal to us. This can be a good thing, but might limit the creation of new ideas for your project. Try these suggestions:

- Talk to other people about what sort of project they might do. Don't ask your friends at school (they might also be finding it difficult to come up with an idea!), but ask your parents, your little brother/sister, your aunt, your grandfather, your neighbour, or someone from a different culture to you. They can't tell you what you must do, but their responses might trigger off some new ideas for you.
- Consider what you might do if you were a different person. For example, if you were David Beckham, Priscilla Chan, or Huda Kattan, what ideas might you have? Or if you were a police officer or a dentist, what ideas might you have? It doesn't matter who it is, you're just trying to change your usual perspective and look at things a little differently.

Random choice

You need to look for different stimuli to help you come up with some ideas. Open a dictionary or a web page, select a word at random. Look for possible connections between this word and a possible topic. Look through some photos in a magazine – does one of those get you thinking of different ideas? Can one of these be developed into a project idea that would really interest you?

Ideas shower: generating ideas

Everyone needs to be clear about the rules for generating ideas. To be successful, an ideas shower session has to be structured.

- Start with a goal: set yourself an objective for your session.
- Time your session, about 10-20 minutes. If you need it to go on longer than this, have a break first.
- Generate ideas in a place where you know you will be relaxed, it could be somewhere you don't normally work.
- Always have a pen and paper, a flip chart or a whiteboard to jot down all your ideas. A group may have a scribe whose only role is to record the ideas.
- Note every idea that comes into your head: nothing is too stupid to include. In fact, something may initially sound silly but lead onto something good.

1 Project management skills: starting out

Building up an initial project idea

You have by now a much better idea (or ideas) of the topic area for your project. You need to identify the initial idea, and to clarify the planned path or aims and objectives. This path requires you to first identify a 'working title' for your research project. Your Project Supervisor will meet with you to discuss your initial idea(s) and explore your suggested working title.

In order to establish your 'working' title, you will need to undertake some preliminary research. This will help you decide on the resources where you will start your research, and have clear aims and objectives. Identify your project's aims and objectives

Your working title or objective must have a clear focus. You will present it as part of the Project Proposal Form and give it a title. This title should be a single phrase presenting the topic succinctly and clearly. It may be a short statement, a question, or a hypothesis. Any one of these may look to solve a problem, seek to confirm or deny a theory, or suggest an investigation to explore an issue. Avoid any title that would lead to a largely descriptive report. You must set up an investigation or argument with more than one view to be analysed. Previous examples of titles have included:

- Concrete or asphalt for motorway surfaces?
- The Trojan Horse: Fact or Fiction?
- How has English affected the German language? Is this leading to its decline as a world language?

Your aims and objectives will include your proposed action, that is, the key tasks you consider necessary to fulfil the project outline as well as the format for the presentation for your project.

These should be clear and focused. You need to be able to complete them within the time you have available, and to write about your topic within the Oxford AQA Exams word limit.

Can you explain your project to others? Share your project title, aims and objectives with another student. You are well on the way if you can explain why you are carrying out this project, what it will be called, and what you hope to achieve in terms of its aims and objectives.

Key term

'Working' title This is the title you start with, and that is agreed as part of your proposal with your Supervisor.

Word limit You must submit a written report which is 5000 words long (+/- 10%). This means that you must write more than 4500, but no more than 5500 words.

Study tip

Your working title and your proposed action must allow you to investigate and access all the skills that you see in the Assessment Objectives. So the scope of your project must allow you to plan, research, analyse, and evaluate your topic, not just describe or narrate the topic.

From 'working' title to final title

The initial idea(s) for your project and your project aims and objectives will be summed up in your 'working' title. This 'working' title is agreed with your Supervisor. You will have done some preliminary research into your topic which helps you develop this 'working' title.

At your mid-project review meeting held with your Supervisor (see chapter x in this book), you will be expected to show how you have completed your research, before moving on to the report-writing stage. Your plan may have changed at this point, depending on how your project work has progressed. As a result of your meeting with your Supervisor, you may make modifications to your plan. This is not a problem. In fact, it's a very acceptable part of project research.

You will record these changes (or modifications) in your Production Log. You will also decide on your 'final' title. This may be a bit different from your original 'working' title. Again, this is not a problem, since it reflects the nature of independent research. Remember the assessment of your IPQ is very focused on the process you follow, as well as your final written report.

Study tip

You may choose to work up more than one initial idea for your meeting with your Supervisor. Or if your Supervisor doesn't agree that your first initial idea will work effectively as a research project, you may need to work through more than one initial idea. This is not a problem, and is all part of the learning and research process. Consider your Supervisor as helping you to achieve the best results in your project research. Their advice is a valuable resource for you.

1 Project management skills: starting out

Working independently

Completing your IPQ gives you the opportunity to choose your own topic of study and work on your own. This is great preparation for employment or higher education. It may also be one of the first times where you've had to take responsibility for your own work at this level.

> **ACTIVITY Independent working**
>
> **1** Independent working has its own risks. Read the statements A–E below, then decide your level of experience of these risk factors (where 1 = no experience at all; 2 = some experience, and 3 = lots of experience). On the right, write a number 1–3 and note how you intend to overcome these risk factors.
>
> A believing you have lots more time than you do, particularly at the start
>
> B not structuring and planning your time in detail
>
> C missing key deadlines
>
> D not giving yourself key deadlines, or monitoring your progress against your plan
>
> E not asking for advice and support from the right people

> **Study tip**
>
> Working independently does not mean you are on your own. Your Project Supervisor will schedule key meetings with you, and will be available at other times to offer advice, guidance and support. If your Supervisor can't help you, they'll be able to suggest other people who can.

Checklist: are you ready for your initial ideas review meeting with your Supervisor?

As part of your IPQ, you are required to gain Oxford AQA Exams approval for your project title.

Your Supervisor will discuss with you exactly how to go about getting your project approved. Work through your initial idea(s) with your Supervisor to get some early feedback.

> **Study tip**
>
> Make sure you can 'sell' your project idea to your Supervisor. Practise describing it in one or two sentences so that it sounds succinct and clear. If you can convince yourself that it's something you are passionate about and that you can research it in sufficient depth (at A level standard), your Supervisor will appreciate this and be able to help you more easily to gain approval for your project title.

You need to be sure that your idea has sufficient potential for you to fulfill the Assessment Objectives effectively. Use this checklist to make sure you're prepared to meet your Supervisor.[1]

	Yes	No	If no, why not? Comment on your next steps
I have a clear idea of how completing an IPQ will be of benefit to me			
I have carefully considered the time I need to make available for completing my Independent Project			
I have thought carefully about my topic area and know it really interests me			
I have considered what resources I have available and to what extent this impacts on my topic choice			

---

[1] Filling in this chart is not an Oxford AQA Exams requirement for your IPQ. However it may help you to prepare for a meeting with your Supervisor.

1 Project management skills: starting out

	Yes	No	If no, why not? Comment on your next steps
I have given sufficient thought to my suggested project title(s) and feel confident it will give me scope to fulfil the assessment criteria			
I have a good idea of the financial costs involved with carrying out my project and have considered if this affects my topic choice			
I've drawn up at least one draft project title (my suggested 'working title')			
I have done some preliminary research to help me decide on my project title and the initial resources where i will start my researchI've got a good idea of my project aims and objectives			
My project title allows me to make use of high-level research skills including planning, analysis, evaluation and explanation			
The questions I need to ask my Supervisor in my initial planning meeting are:			
As a result of my meeting with my Project Supervisor, I need to:			

1 Project management skills: starting out

Initial planning for your project

By the end of this section, you should be able to:
- ✔ explore the tasks and sub-tasks involved in the work of your project
- ✔ identify the timings involved in each phase of the project
- ✔ understand a variety of project planning techniques available to you
- ✔ draft an initial plan for your project.

Project planning

A project is more likely to be successful if you do some research before you start. You need to identify the sort of tasks you need to do, and whom or where you will consult in order to fulfil your objectives. This planning process will allow you to anticipate the risks involved and the problems you might face, and to manage your project efficiently.

Project planning techniques are useful in many different situations, such as planning a holiday, a gap year, a revision programme or a work-related task. A thorough plan helps you to make sure that your goals are achievable within the time and budget you have available.

> **Study tip**
>
> The most common comment offered by students when they reflect on the work of their Independent Project is:
>
> *'If I did this again I would plan my time better.'*

What factors do you need to consider?

Several different factors will impact on the successful completion of your project. These might include the following.

- **Time available:** work back from your final deadline, and include any interim dates you need to meet. Also consider other commitments in and out of school, and deadlines for other subjects. What time do you have to do the required tasks? How much time will each task take? To keep yourself on track, break your project into a series of phases with short-term deadlines.
- **Resources available:** What sources are available, are there enough to cover your research topic? Do you need any specialist equipment or materials in order to gather your own primary data? Are these all readily available in your school, or do you need to find them yourself?

> **Key term**
>
> **Project plan** This is a project schedule which details the key tasks and the deadlines you need to achieve to fulfil your project.

- **Dependencies:** work out the sequence of tasks to be carried out. Note which tasks can only be done once a preceding task has been completed. This is the critical path of your project plan. It highlights the items in your schedule which could hold up the remaining phases of the project. For example, you can't hold an event such as a football match unless you have found somewhere to play. The timing f when some other tasks are done may not be so critical to the success of the project.
- **Risks or potential problems:** what could go wrong? Might problems get in your way? Does your plan rely too heavily on a busy person's contribution? Do you need some 'buffer' time or contingency, in case problems arise?

Checklist for successful project planning

Clear goals: write down exactly what it is you are hoping to achieve.

Communication: work out how and when you will communicate with other people involved in or interested in your project's progress.

Risk management: carry out a risk assessment to stay safe, (see page 62); anticipate any other potential problems and create a 'plan B' should these occur.

Keep realistic: be entirely realistic about the resources you have: stay rational and down-to-earth about the schedule and scope of the project.

Keep on track: identify exactly how you will keep to the deadlines you have set yourself, and monitor your own progress.

Clearly define roles and responsibilities: if your project involves other people (you might interview them, for example), make sure they are clear about what, how, and when they should help you.

Making a diary

Making a print or electronic diary is essential to planning your own time, keeping you on track, and reducing the risks of working independently. This diary does not need to be submitted but you might want to include a sample page or two as evidence of your organisation skills to complement the production log entries.

- ✔ At the start, put in all your appointments with your Project Supervisor.
- ✔ Put in your key project dates as outlined in your own project plan.
- ✔ Include all the Oxford AQA Exams deadlines (your Supervisor will know them).
- ✔ Add other activities in your project plan, showing when they have to be done and completed.
- ✔ Plan time for fun and rest as well!
- ✔ Keep your diary with you always – and refer to it regularly.
- ✔ Set up phone alerts or email reminders to warn you of key dates and what needs to be done.

1 Project management skills: starting out

For project planning techniques see pages 30–31.

ACTIVITY Project planning

As part of a school charity day, there will be a 'table top' sale. You will be selling second-hand books. You have been asked to market the event around school. You have to produce 200 leaflets to distribute in the staff room, classrooms, the library, and promote the event online. You have three weeks to fulfil the brief.

Using one of the project planning techniques described overleaf, or one of your own:
1. Break down this project into smaller tasks and estimate the time needed for each task.
2. Identify the dependencies – that is, which tasks can only be done when another has been completed.
3. Prepare a project plan.
4. Is it all manageable within the time and money resources you have available? If not, what changes do you need to make?

What this means for my project

This type of project planning is vital for the successful development of your Independent Project. At the same time, your Project Proposal Form requires you to complete a Planning review. On the form, you need to list:

- the research/activity/task to be carried out and the deadlines you set yourself
- the sources you will consult in your research (these might involve you accessing
- library resources, an online database, or carrying out some face to face interviews)
- your proposed actions.

Study tip

Your Project Proposal Form requires you to list any likely resources you will make use of in your project work. It's helpful, therefore, to make a note of any books, websites, data or evidence you refer to in your initial planning which may be relevant for your project. This represents good practice for when you move on to your full research anyway. You are also asked to append any planning documentation or tools that you may use. The main elements of the plan need to be in the log. Additional planning materials should be minimal, and not all submitted with the final project

Project planning techniques

There are several project planning tools and techniques you can use.

Planning with Gantt charts

A Gantt chart is a useful tool to help schedule actions and tasks which are part of a project that has a number of stages. A Gantt chart is a horizontal bar chart showing the scheduled tasks and dependencies against a timeline. It will:

- ✔ help you to break down tasks into smaller chunks of work
- ✔ assist in working out a critical path for a project
- ✔ help you to plan for periods of more intense activity
- ✔ help you to monitor progress and check whether you are on schedule or not.

To create a Gantt chart

1. Make a list of all the activities you think will form part of the project you need to plan. Be as comprehensive as you can.
2. List the length of time you think each task should take. Work out which tasks must precede (come before) others, and which tasks can be done in parallel.
3. Using spreadsheet software, list the days/ weeks/months you have available to complete your project across the horizontal (x) axis.
4. Down the vertical (y)axis, list all the activities in the correct order of completion. Then draw a horizontal bar beside each task to represent the length of time it will take.

Planning with sticky notes

This can be a very practical way to visualise the tasks you have ahead.

1. List all the tasks and sub-tasks that make up your project and write each one of them on a sticky note. At this point, you just need to list everything. Don't worry about getting them in the right order.
2. Now group the sticky notes together into larger areas of activity. Write how long each task should take on each sticky note.
3. On a whiteboard, create a start point on the left and an end point on the right. Place the sticky notes in a logical line, drawing a line into each activity box (or sticky note) and a line out. This will help you identify dependencies.

Using online planning templates

You can also find free planning templates online; these provide a structure which you can personalise for your own needs. (Free or open source project planning software may also be available online, but remember these are often set up for multi-user team projects so are perhaps more complex than you need now.)

1 Project management skills: starting out

Drawing up a detailed project plan

Having looked at the different project planning techniques available to you, you should now be able to consider your own project in more detail and create your own project plan. In some cases, you may need to carry out this detailed planning before your project can be approved. In other cases, your initial planning may provide sufficient information for your proposal to be approved.

> **Key term**
>
> **Dependencies** The tasks that have to be done first in order that other tasks can be done. For example, are there materials you need before you can start an experiment for your research?

Your plan

Your plan will need to detail the following.
1. **Main tasks** involved in carrying out your project.
2. **Sub-tasks** related to these main tasks.
3. **Critical path** of your project: what are the dependencies?
4. **Time you have available**: the deadline for submission, as well as interim project requirements are laid down by Oxford International AQA Exams; your school may also set deadlines for you.
5. **Time that each task and sub-task will take**.
6. **Risks** that might be involved during your project, together with a plan of action should they materialise.
7. **Budget** (if applicable) that you are working to.
8. How often will you **communicate**/meet up with your Project Supervisor?
9. **Format** to present your project.
10. **How you will monitor your own progress** against the project plan. This is a very important part of your project plan and should include all relevant details. For example, what sort of checks will you put in place to ensure that you're on target to achieve your objectives? How will you know that each element of your project is being given the appropriate amount of time, and that you will finish it on schedule? If you have to divert from the original plan, perhaps for good reason, what will you do?

> **ACTIVITY Drawing up a plan**
>
> Using one of the techniques described above, draw up an initial plan for your own Independent Project

> **Study tip**
>
> You are more likely to have success in the IPQ if you have a detailed project plan, and can provide clear evidence of how you will monitor your progress against the agreed project plan, even if you later change this plan. You will achieve a lower grade if your project plan is brief, with little evidence of how you will keep track of your project's development.

Organisational skills – keeping your project on track

Of course, coming up with a good project plan is not all of it. It's a great start – and absolutely essential. You've also got to keep track of progress and ensure you're on schedule to succeed.

> **ACTIVITY Personal organisational skills audit**
>
> **1** Identify a project or a task you completed recently. It may be related to school work, or something in your free time. Write down what it was.
>
>   **A** Make a note of all the skills you used really well to carry out this task.
>
>   **B** Make a note of all the skills you could have improved in order to do this task better.
>
> **2** Define the organisational skills you believe are necessary for successful completion of your project. Write these down, dividing up your ideas into:
>
>   **A** those which are a 'must-have' or essential
>
>   **B** those which are a 'nice to have' or desirable

> **ACTIVITY Matching competencies and skills requirements**
>
> **1** How do your own competencies match up to the skills requirements listed on page 33? Decide what level of experience you have in these areas. Write a number 1–3 beside each list item, according to the following levels:
>
>   **A** no experience at all = 1
>
>   **B** some experience = 2
>
>   **C** lots of experience = 3
>
> **2** In the areas where you have no experience or very little, consider what you will do to compensate for this or how you will work differently with regard to your Independent Project. Your Supervisor might be able to help here.

> **Key term**
>
> **Competence** (competencies - pl) the ability or talent to do something very well or very efficiently
>
> **Critical path** the sequence of tasks in your project which need the longest time and will affect the end date (or deadline) if they are delayed. Some tasks may be done later, but won't necessarily impact on the end date; these don't form part of the critical path.

Organisational skills for the purposes of your Independent Project involve three key areas.

Managing your time

We often hear the phrase 'time management', but we can't manage time, only the activities we do within that time.

- ✔ Plan out each task and sub task to be completed by a particular date. ☐
- ✔ Plan your time so that you know exactly when you will be working on your Extended Project. ☐
- ✔ Protect this planned time carefully. ☐
- ✔ Carry out tasks in the most effective order, and always be aware of the critical path of your project. ☐

Managing yourself

- ✔ Start with a positive commitment to fulfil your Independent Project. ☐
- ✔ It is very easy to get distracted – developing self-discipline is crucial. (Put your phone in a different room when you work on your project!) ☐
- ✔ List the tasks you will do at the beginning of each planned period of work; short term goals are as important as long term goals. ☐
- ✔ Learn to adjust or amend your plans as required. Keep a record of the changes you make and why you made them. ☐
- ✔ Build in rewards for completing some of your goals. ☐

Managing your environment

- ✔ Re-adjust others' expectations of you and what free time you will have available. ☐
- ✔ Identify where you work best, both at school and at home. ☐
- ✔ Organise your desk so that you are working most effectively. ☐
- ✔ Organise your files on your computer and regularly make a back up of all your work. ☐
- ✔ Make your notes on A4 punched paper so you can easily file them in a ring binder and organise/index them appropriately. ☐
- ✔ User a planner, diary or calendar to assign time to tasks. ☐

Project proposal and approval

By the end of this section, you should:
- ✔ understand what is involved in the project approval process and why it matters
- ✔ appreciate what your Project Supervisor needs to consider when assessing your project idea
- ✔ be able to prepare for your planning review meeting with your Project Supervisor.
- ✔ What is involved in the project approval process?

Oxford AQA has a formal project approval process which you need to be aware of. This process helps you and your Supervisor make sure that you have chosen an appropriate area of study and project objectives. This is a check that you will be able to fulfil the assessment criteria and achieve success. Your Project Supervisor will support you through this process, but it is important that you understand the requirements. See the Oxford International AQA specification[2].

Checklist for the approval of titles

Your Supervisor will need to check the following:
- ✔ Your project topic allows for the development and extension of your skills and knowledge outside of your other areas of study.
- ✔ Your project allows you to access the higher level concepts and skills in the assessment objectives, that is that you can plan, research, analyse, evaluate, and explain – rather than simply describe and narrate.
- ✔ Your project title is clear and focussed on a specific issue which will allow you to fulfil it within the timescale and within the word limits, and that it will not end up either too long or too short.
- ✔ Your project title will allow you to work independently, investigating and researching your objectives without having to rely on a very small number of existing resources which would limit the potential for original work.
- ✔ You will be able to approach your project impartially and in an entirely balanced way.
- ✔ You have a good idea of the format and date of presentation of your final project.

[2] Please refer to the current version of the specification on Oxford International AQA's website at www.oxfordaqaexams.org.uk/subjects/projects/ipq

Checklist: are you ready for your Planning Review meeting?

Use this checklist to make sure you're appropriately prepared[3].

	My notes
I have carefully considered which topic area I'd like to form the basis of my research, and it is …	
My project title is …	
I have conducted preliminary research into possible sources and know where I can find relevant information (see page 43 onwards for more information on research methods).	
The way this project allows me to fulfil the assessment criteria is …	
The way I will monitor my progress against my project plan is …	
I have carried out a skills audit and considered the risks involved in organising my project and available time are …	
I have begun to think about the risks involved in gathering the data I need (see page 62).	
I will manage time and resources as part of my project plan by …	
The issues involved with working independently are…	
The time I have available is …	
The questions to ask my Project Supervisor in my Planning Review meeting are…	
What else do I need to do?	

What this means for my project

The work of this chapter allows you and your Project Supervisor to complete parts A and B of the AQA Project Proposal Form. Part C of this form will also be completed by your Centre Coordinator. Once this is done, your project proposal has been formally approved. Completed Parts A, B and C of the Project Proposal Form form part of the evidence required for assessment and moderation. Once your project proposal has been formally approved, you will then have a planning review meeting with your Supervisor.

---

[3]Filling in this chart is not an Oxford AQA Exams requirement for your IPQ. However it may help you to prepare for a meeting with your Supervisor.

Project progress checkpoint

▼ 1 Project management skills: starting out

Have you completed part A of the Project Proposal Form?	Yes No
Have you discussed the Project Proposal Form, and in particular, part B of the Form with your Supervisor?	Yes No
Have you got all the information you need regarding the approval process within your part ?	Yes No

▶ 2 Project management skills: researching the project

▶ 3 Project management skills: producing the project product

▶ 4 Presenting your project

▶ 5 Finalising and submitting your project

▶▶▶ Next steps

The next stage of your Independent Project Qualification is to really focus on the research for your project. As a result of discussions with your Project Supervisor in your planning review meeting, you might choose to make amendments or changes to your project plan. This is not a problem; you just need to record the changes you make. Your project research will involve using resources effectively, and the development of skills such as critical thinking, decision making, and problem solving to support you in the successful completion of this stage.

Project management skills: researching the project | 2

Now you have an approved project title and a plan, you need to concentrate on researching information and developing new skills. Skills and techniques may be introduced as part of the taught element of the IPQ course. The skills introduced in this chapter are likely to be useful to most students – you should take the opportunity to understand and apply them whatever the subject area of your project.

> **This chapter will help you to:**
> ✔ refine your project plan in the light of your Project proposal meeting, and prepare for your Planning Review meeting
> ✔ apply different research techniques and use resources effectively
> ✔ reference resources appropriately in line with academic protocols
> ✔ use the Internet effectively as a research tool
> ✔ use technology appropriately to support and benefit your research
> ✔ prepare for your mid-term review.

Taught element

On the whole, your project involves you working independently, with some individual supervision and guidance from your Project Supervisor. The IPQ also requires the teaching of specific research skills (eg project planning, how to avoid plagiarism, or report writing). Your school is likely to teach you these skills in lessons or in library time. This is called the 'taught element' of the IPQ.

Staying still gets you nowhere.

2 Project management skills: researching the project

Project management

By the end of this section, you should be able to:
- ✔ review your project plan having discussed this with your Supervisor
- ✔ link your project work, including the development of new skills, to IPQ assessment criteria.

Review your project plan

As a result of discussions with your Project Supervisor at your planning review meeting, you may now wish to revise your plan.

Remember that planning is a key part of the success of your Independent Project Qualification and being awarded a good grade. You should avoid rushing into the research and final production without being clear about your plan.

Your Project Supervisor may meet with you to discuss how you have reviewed your plan. You need to record any comments or advice from your Project Supervisor or your Centre Coordinator (where appropriate), and how you will implement their recommendations, and why (or why not).

You should also think about the research methods you are going to use – see page 43.

Study tip

You should now complete page 12 of the Oxford International AQA Candidate Record Form where you need to detail any changes, clarifications or additions as a result of advice from your Project Supervisor, Centre Coordinator, and your Specialist Consultant (if you have one).

What sort of skills will I need to develop?

Part of your Independent Project Qualification will be delivered in class time, where you will be taught the skills you need to complete your project Most centres will devote about 30 hours of teaching time to introduce you to skills that are useful to most students. If you need additional specialist skills, then your Project Supervisor will advise you on the best way to go about developing these skills.

Assessment for the IPQ will look at the evidence you can provide of the skills you have learned and developed through the entire project. The Oxford International AQA IPQ specification outlines how the assessment objectives are weighted[1]:

- Ten per cent (10%) weighting of the assessment is for how well you select an area of interest and establish a working title so that your project has clear aims and objectives, and makes use of appropriate resources
- Twenty per cent (20%) weighting of the assessment is for how well you create a project plan (including a time schedule), that you undertake a risk assessment, and track your progress against the objectives you set
- Twenty per cent (20%) weighting of the assessment is for the skills you demonstrate to research, select, organise, and investigate a range of information, and how you justify the range of any primary and secondary sources used
- Forty per cent (40%) weighting of the assessment is for how well you implement your project plan, analyse your research findings, and organise these findings in a 5000 word report, making appropriate use of references and a bibliography. You will communicate a conclusion and your outcomes in both your report and your live presentation.
- A further 10% weighting of the assessment relates to how you evaluate the strengths and weaknesses of the project process and your report, as well as review your own learning.

Not all the skills you are taught will be immediately relevant. The ability to reflect on what you have learned, then select and apply the skills needed for your project, is critical to a successful Independent Project.

The Assessment Objectives table on the next pages shows how individual skills are assessed, and how you can achieve a good grade.

> **Key term**
>
> **Review your learning** Careful thought and consideration of what you are taught, and deciding if it is useful or relevant to your needs.

---

[1] Please refer to the current version of the IPQ specification published by Oxford International AQA exams at www.oxfordaqaexams.org.uk/subjects/projects/ipq

2 Project management skills: researching the project

Oxford AQA assessment objectives

Assessment Objective	What this involves	Weighting
AO1 Selection of topic	• Identify and select the area of interest you want to research • Devise the aims and objectives for your project • Establish a working title, by doing some preliminary research and using a selection of appropriate sources	10%
	What should I do to achieve the higher grades? You need to make it clear what your area of study is and write a concise title and project aims and objectives. The more precise titles help students focus on what they are aiming to achieve. It doesn't matter if you have to refine your working title into something slightly different (ie your final title) as your project progresses. Your working title needs to be able to allow you to investigate and to access the higher level concepts and skills in the assessment objectives, so that you can analyse and evaluate your findings, rather than simply describe and narrate them.	
AO2 Planning, monitoring and developing	• Produce a project plan which includes a schedule detailing the tasks you will do and when you will do them • Carry out a risk assessment to assess the health, safety, and risk issues associated with your project • Monitor your progress against the objectives you set yourself making sure that you explain why you are choosing the tasks you plan and justifying any changes you make in the light of experience during your project	20%
	What should I do to achieve the higher grades? Your project plan should be very detailed with clear evidence of how you will monitor progress against your project plan. Your monitoring techniques should be justified (eg using a particular project management technique).	
AO3 Demonstration of research skills	• Research a range of different information and resources appropriate to your research • Select the most appropriate resources for you to use • Examine the resources critically • Organise the information and resources you gather • Justify the selection of any secondary and primary resources you use	20%
	What should I do to achieve the higher grades? Make sure you select and evaluate a wide range of relevant sources. As you find relevant information and data, analyse it critically and comment on its validity or how it relates to other research in this topic area. Make sure you have a clear and justified purpose for the sources you use. Relate the information and data to your own project, by relating it to your own ideas and how you intend to develop your project. Be systematic and well organised in how you gather information and reference your sources, so that you can create a comprehensive bibliography later on.	

AO4 Analysis and application of research	• Implement the project plan • Analyse the findings of the project research • Arrange these findings in a 5000 word report • Include a conclusion to your report and communicate your outcomes • Include a bibliography and references and any other appropriate appendices to your report • Decide on an appropriate format for your presentation (in line with any school requirements you might have) • Deliver your presentation and answer the follow-up questions from the audience or your Supervisor	40%
	What should I do to achieve the higher grades? Your project plan is implemented clearly throughout. Your written report is of an appropriate length and writing style with a clear focus on your title. You analyse your research findings thoroughly and communicate them clearly in the report. You have a good grasp of your subject, and you have created a compelling report and presentation with a well evidenced conclusion. You organise your project well, and reference all your sources appropriately. Where you have to change your project plan or you adapt your working title (or your aims and objective), make sure you provide clear reasons and explanations for these changes.	
AO5 Evaluation of product, process and self	• Evaluate the strengths and weaknesses of the project process (including a review of your own learning) and your report	10%
	What should I do to achieve the higher grades? Provide a detailed and careful evaluation of the strengths and weaknesses of your completed project. This should relate to both your final report and the organisation of your project. Evaluate the process you carried out and reflect on your own learning with detailed understanding. Make sure all your material is relevant, well structured and appropriately presented.	

2 Project management skills: researching the project

The grading process

The IPQ is graded as a whole and not marked. Before you can be awarded any grade, you have to provide each of the following elements (or evidence that they have been done). If any student fails to supply one of the following, they will be allocated a U (= ungraded):

- You identify and select an area of interest (and provide evidence in the Production Log).
- You set a working title (and provide evidence in the Production Log).
- You carry out a risk assessment (your Supervisor confirms this in the Production Log)
- You produce a project plan (and provide evidence in the Production Log).
- You implement the project plan and record any changes you make to it (and provide evidence in the Production Log).
- You produce a report addressing your final title of 5000 words (+/− 10%)
- You use a referencing method in your written report.
- You communicate your research findings in the report and in the live presentation.
- You create a bibliography/reference list (included in your report and as an appendix).
- You evaluate the strengths and weaknesses of the project (and provide evidence in the Production Log).

Supervisors and your Centre Coordinator are responsible for the internal assessment of all projects. They follow a very rigorous, accurate, and consistent process to grade each project. There are six grades awarded, A*, A, B, C, D, and E, as in all A-levels. Once the grade has been determined, the Supervisor records this with their comments in the Production Log. Working to standards set by Oxford AQA Examinations, all projects are internally moderated. This ensures that all grades are awarded fairly and consistently.

Your Supervisor might read a draft of your report, but they can only give a grade to the final project report. Once the report has been graded, you cannot get it back to rewrite or improve it.

Research methods

> **By the end of this section, you should be able to:**
> ✔ identify and evaluate the most valuable resources for your project
> ✔ use the Internet effectively as a research tool
> ✔ establish codes of conduct if using people in your research
> ✔ recognise links in your research
> ✔ record and reference your resources to fulfil the assessment criteria

This section is about researching information and evaluating what you find. Before you start, think carefully about:
- what information you need for your project
- what sort of information
- how much information.

To answer this you need to think about how your findings will relate to the topic of your project, and the way you intend to structure your project report and/or the nature of your artefact.

Supporting your ideas with research

Think about the type of data and resources which would inform your thinking about your project. Try to develop your own ideas through an understanding of similar work already done. This does not mean your ideas will not be 'original'. It just means they are well-informed and evidence-based, and that your proposals or statements are backed up by evidence.

As an example, imagine a group of organisations competing to design a skate park for teenagers. No matter how imaginative, fun and attractive the designs, no-one will be impressed if the design is not backed up by research. In this case research might be around durability of materials and surfaces, national safety standards, recent developments in skate parks ll over the world, how people use skate parks, environmental factors and views of local residents.

Key questions for research

By now you will have a title for your project, which may or may not be a question but should certainly set up something to investigate, compare or analyse. It is very important to give enough thought to your title, since your whole project depends on this.

To decide on what research is needed, you need to focus on the key questions about your project topic.

For instance, what questions might the designers have asked about skate parks? Examples might be: 'What are the most up-to-date surfaces being used in this country and abroad?' What UK safety standards do we need to adhere to?

> **ACTIVITY Focussing the questions for your research**
>
> Write down your project title, then write down three questions relevant to your research. These questions must be interesting enough to keep you motivated, and must be possible to answer within the time frame.
>
> Now list possible sources of information relevant to each question, including any primary data you need to collect.
>
> Explain how each information source will help you to answer your research questions.
>
> Swap your questions and ideas for information sources with another student, and share some constructive criticism on each other's work.

Identifying likely resources

Sources of information to answer the question about safety standards for skate parks might be government reports and other documents, survey data, academic articles and reports.

Other sources relevant to your project will depend on the topic, but might include publications such as reports, articles, books and newspapers, archives or geographical data. Secondary data products such as census data, longitudinal data sets or survey data might be used. In addition, you might collect your own data (primary data).

The sheer quantity and ease of access to information means that it is important to use effective searching strategies, then evaluate what you find. To support your research, you should look for professional and reliable information online, and also:

- in libraries (school, public, or those within universities if these are available to you)
- in archives of professional institutions
- amongst local professionals or employers: you or your school may have already formed relationships with local organisations through work experience or voluntary work
- from charities and voluntary organisations.

The next section is about consulting a range of resources, including text books, the British Library, online journals, experts in the field, and surveys.

> **ACTIVITY Books and journals**
>
> 1. Visit your school library and locate any textbooks for your project area. Familiarise yourself with the books available, so you know where to look for information you might need in the future. Look up one key term relevant to your current study in the index of a selected book. Note the book title, author and page number, along with one new fact you have discovered on that page.
> 2. Locate one text book relevant to your project topic. Find the ISBN number on the back of this book. Find out what ISBN stands for, and how this number might be useful to you.
> 3. What type of publication has an ISSN (International Standard Serial Number)? Who issues ISSN numbers?
> 4. The British Library holds 14 million books, 920,000 journal and newspaper titles, 58 million patents, 3 million sound recordings, and a lot more – so this represents a vast potential resource for you. Some of it is available online; go to the home page of the British Library. Click on 'About the British Library', then click on 'Quick Information'. This will show you what you can do on their websites.

Evaluating your resources

Because of the vast range of information available, it is important that you learn to evaluate the usefulness and reliability of sources. You might, for example, be able to rapidly identify a source as relatively unreliable. This helps you to use your research time more efficiently.

There is a range of criteria you might refer to when judging a source's reliability:

- **Reliability of the author** – Who is the author? What is the professional background of the author? What year was the information written? What is their occupation? Are they sponsored or supported by an organisation that has a vested interest?
- **Reliability of publisher** – What is the purpose of the resource? Is it to persuade or to inform? Who is the target audience?
- **Reliability of cited sources** – Can you trust the sources listed in the bibliography?
- **Reliability of information sources** – Is there a comprehensive peer review policy? Who are the experts quoted? Is the information complete and coherent? For example, do conclusions match the data that has been presented? Does the source present a balanced view or is there evidence of bias?

> **Key term**
>
> **Peer review** A peer review is where an author's work is reviewed by other academic or professional people working in the same field. This suggests that the work has been 'endorsed' or verified by someone who is qualified to know.

2 Project management skills: researching the project

ACTIVITY

The following table summarises some criteria you could take into account when deciding whether or not the information you have researched is reliable. The table has statements missing in one or other of the two columns. What are the missing statements needed to complete the table?

Remember that you also need to assess whether the information is useful for your project, and whether it is at the right level for you.

About the author of the work

Likely to be reliable	Problematic
Recognised experts	
Work in a respected institution	Not connected with any recognised institution or organisation
No commercial or academic interest in the issues	

The publication

Likely to be reliable	Problematic
Reputable journal where articles are peer reviewed	
	Source which may have a strong commitment to one point of view or motive
Recent (is this always an advantage?)	
	Produced in a country with political restrictions

Data

Likely to be reliable	Problematic
The difference between the intervention and the control group is large enough to be statistically significant	
	Small sample size
Unbiased sample: participants involved are placed in the intervention and control group randomly	
	Data collected from a group or situation which can't be generalised to the situation of interest to your project

Conclusions

Likely to be reliable	Problematic
Conclusions are backed up by the evidence	
There is an accepted mechanism to explain the conclusion.	Data might be explained in another way
	The conclusions are based only on a correlation

Checklist for evaluating your sources

Use the following checklist of questions for three resources that you have already collected.

1. How is the source relevant to your project? Is it at the right level?
2. What conclusions are suggested by the headline or introduction?
3. Who carried out any research that is being reported, and what is their reputation?
4. Who paid for the report or investigation?
5. Was any data collection or investigation carried out?
6. Where were the outcomes of research reported?
7. What do other experts in the field say about the research or report?
8. Would you be able to make a decision based on these resources? How might you get more information?
9. Is the source current/up-to-date? Does that matter? (An historic source might be appropriate if your topic concerns something which happened in the past.)

ACTIVITY Academic referees

1 Nature is an international science journal, but the same principles apply in other subject areas.

Look up the 'guide for referees' web page on the Nature website.

A Make a note of brief definitions for the following terms:
- peer–reviewer
- independent reviewer

B Save the 'criteria for publication' and 'The review process' (on their 'Peer-review policy' page) for use in question 2 on the next page.

Based on Learning Skills for Science and reproduced by permission of Gatsby Technical Education Projects.

2 Project management skills: researching the project

Wikipedia

Wikipedia is a source of vast amounts of information, but is viewed with suspicion because of the way it is produced. Entries on the site can be written by anybody. Although there is some attempt to prevent false information being posted, there is no formal peer-review process. Many of the Wikipedia entries have extensive bibliographies (sometimes listed under 'References' or 'Notes'). This is an indication that many authors are using a range of information sources to back up what they write. Does this mean that it is a reliable source of information?

It is likely that you should only use Wikipedia as a source of links to useful material, not as a source in its own right. If you do use and reference material directly from Wikipedia, make sure you evaluate it in the same way as any other source.

ACTIVITY Wikipedia

1. Choose an article on Wikipedia with some relevance to your topic area, and make an assessment of how reliable you think it is. You should carefully read the text for evidence of bias and any gaps in the content that you think should be filled. You should also look at the sources which are referenced, to see if a broad range of sources have been considered by the author. Are the sources reliable in their own right?

2. Use the 'criteria for publication' from the Nature journal to decide if you would 'accept', 'ask for revisions' or 'reject outright' this article if you were on the editorial board of a journal like Nature. Make a note of your reasons.

Based on Learning Skills for Science and reproduced by permission of Gatsby Technical Education Projects.

Using the Internet effectively as a research tool

You are probably already familiar with using the Internet for researching information. You may be a regular user of Google, for example, to search on specific key terms. But have you ever had any formal instruction to ensure you are using it effectively? For the purposes of your Independent Project, it is wise to review your use of search engines to ensure you are searching effectively. Google, for example, has a number of additional features:

- If Google is available in your country, you can go to your country's Google site. But you could also access Google for the US or for the UK which may be more useful for your area of interest.
- You could also go to different versions of Google to help you search for particular types of material – eg images, news items, or videos. If you put @ in front of a word, you can search for that word on social media.
- To search for an exact match for the words you are searching on, put them in inverted quotes. For example, "Independent Project".
- If too many options come up for your searched words, you might choose to exclude a word from your search. Use – in front of the word you want to exclude. For example, independent project -management.
- You can also go to the Advanced Search on Google to help refine your results.

Successful searching

One important rule for searching online is to know exactly what you want. The more precise your search terms, the more you will restrict results to what you need. Other tips:

- ✔ Aim for between two and six key words in any search. If you only put in one word, you'll end up with far too many results.
- ✔ Include the most important words first. Many search engines anticipate that the first word you type is the most important one to you.
- ✔ The main results appear in order, according to how often the sites are accessed by users.

Remember that some results (such as those at the top of a Google search) are sponsored results, paid for by commercial organisations.

Evaluating websites

You have access to a volume of information unimaginable 30 years ago. The Internet is the easiest source of a wide range of information, and an important research tool for your project. However there are no checks on its content. The user needs to be able to distinguish between good quality information and rubbish.

You need to:

- evaluate the quality of the information (see page 45)
- ensure that the information is at the right level for your needs.
- keep checking that it is directly relevant to your project: it is easy to become side-tracked by interesting but less relevant information.

The activity on the opposite page is based on Learning Skills for Science and reproduced by permission of Gatsby Technical Education Projects.

2 Project management skills: researching the project

ACTIVITY Evaluating websites

1 Note down one key question related to your project topic. Find three websites which you believe are sources of information that will help you answer this question. Write down the URLs of these websites.

2 Evaluate the usefulness of these websites according to the criteria below, where 1 = most useful, 3 = least useful.

Criteria	Site A	Site B	Site C
Reliability of the author			
Reliability of the publisher			
Whether the information is subject to independent checks			
Presentation of the information (simple/sophisticated)			
Presence of distracting irrelevant information			
Usefulness of the links			
Date of last update			
Ease of access			
Level of difficulty (general use or specialised use)			
Responsibility for the website (Who sponsors it?)			
Relevance of information to your project.			
Sources referenced are just author's own/ sources include those from other experts.			
Website is personal/ commercial/ government/ organisation			
Lack of bias. Only one side of the argument presented/ hidden message present/ trying to persuade you or change your opinion/ some information is purposely omitted			
TOTAL			

3 This sort of grid is useful for evaluating websites. Are there any other criteria you think would be important when evaluating websites for your project?

Using people as subjects in your research

There is a variety of professional codes of practice which provide guidelines and ethical parameters for the behaviour of researchers. These guidelines may be particular to an area of work (such as the American Psychological Association's Ethics Code or the Market Research Society Code of Conduct), but they all aim to keep the individual being interviewed from harm and to protect their confidentiality. The Wellcome Trust offers guidance "*Ensuring your research is ethical*" accessible at wellcome.ac.uk

> ### ACTIVITY Codes of conduct
>
> Research guidelines or codes of conduct in your topic area for using people as subjects for research.
>
> Generally, you need to consider these three areas:
>
> 1. **Confidentiality** – protect the anonymity of your subjects in order to get good quality information and to prevent them from harm. Remember to treat people with sensitivity if asking questions of a personal or controversial nature.
> 2. Allow your subjects to give their **informed consent**. Tell them the purposes of your research, how the information they give you will be used, and how this will be published or made available to others. If you record an interview, tell them who will be listening to the recording. Your subjects should be given the opportunity to withdraw from the research, or to withhold the data relating to them at any point.
> 3. **Assess the risks** of conducting this sort of research. Your school will have their own guidelines regarding contact with people from outside your institution, so make sure you follow these. Also bear in mind the reliability of the information you gather from interviews and questionnaires.

Conducting an effective interview

Before the interview

Write a letter to invite your subject to take part. Explain the purpose of your research, how their personal data will be protected and how it will be used. If you are writing on someone's recommendation, say so. Suggest how they can get back in touch with you to arrange a meeting or, if necessary, a telephone interview.

Draw up a list of questions to guide your interview or discussion: this might be a fixed set of questions that you will be asking all subjects. Alternatively, you may like to leave it a little more 'free' to allow for a discussion rather than an interview.

During the interview

Introduce yourself, explaining the purpose of your interview and how/why you think your subject can be of help. Let them know how long the interview will take. You may choose to make brief notes, or to make an audio recording of the interview so that you can listen more carefully later. It is polite to ask permission from your subject before making a recording.

2 Project management skills: researching the project

After the interview

Review any notes you made during the interview to make sure you have included all the relevant detail. If you do this within a few hours of the interview, it will be fresh in your mind. Always write and thank your interviewee. Let them know how your project progresses and how much you value their contribution. When you've finished your project you could send them a copy of your report, or tell them what the outcome was.

ACTIVITY Questioning style

1 When interviewing others, your technique will help you to collect the information you need without bias. Out of each pair of question phrases below, which one (A or B) would you select as providing a more effective questioning style? Why?

	A	B
1	Explain to me …	Have you got a system of …?
2	Do you believe …?	To what extent do you believe …?
3	Describe the circumstances in more detail.	Are you happy with the circumstances of …?
4	What do you mean?	What exactly do you mean by …?
5	Option 2 is better, don't you think?	Which do you think is the better option?

2 Discuss the effect of each of the following techniques in relation to effective interviewing:

   A Getting the subject's name wrong

   B Frowning at them

   C Looking at them when they are talking

   D Paraphrasing after they have spoken – 'So what you are saying is …?'

   E Interrupting

   F Listening for content and looking for visual clues.

Using questionnaires

What is a questionnaire?

A questionnaire is a set of questions which are phrased so that people can give the sort of information you are looking for. Everyone gets the same questions, so you can compare the answers. They tend to be used when you need responses from a large sample of a population.

Start by thinking about what information you need, and from whom. Make sure that you address the key research questions for your project. What sort of answers are you looking for, and what questions would elicit these?

You won't get useful answers if your questions aren't right. Do not under-estimate the time it will take to get the questions right. Be prepared to have to change them several times.

A small pilot may be useful. Try out the questions on people who don't know anything about your project - this will tell you whether the questions are the right ones.

What should a questionnaire be like?

The first questions usually provide information about the participant (gender, age, profession, and so on), so you can link the data to the type of person. Put questions which need more thought at the end. The shorter your questionnaire, the more likely people are to fill it in for you. Respondents may not want to take any more than 3-4 minutes on an online survey, for example.

Yes/No answers and answers on a given scale of responses (e.g. 5 is high and 1 is low in a scale of how much you like a flavour of ice-cream) make questionnaires quicker to fill in. It is also easier to analyse this type of quantitative (numerical) data.

Make sure each question only asks for one piece of information. Make your questions clear and specific. ('Do you eat ice cream regularly?' may end up with lots of different interpretations of 'regularly'.)

If you want more subtle and individual responses, you may include open-ended free response questions (such as 'Give an example of an ice-cream that changed your life'). This type of qualitative (subjective or descriptive) data is harder to answer and harder to analyse, but may give more valuable information. You can limit the range of responses to qualitative questions by providing possible answers to choose from (multiple choice responses).

Using interviews

If you want answers to more probing or difficult questions, consider using face to face interviews. Interviewers can still use well-designed questions, but you can follow up unexpected or interesting responses. Interviewing is more time consuming than using a questionnaire, so this method may limit your sample size.

Recording your notes: when interviewing people you can use a recording app on your phone. Give each sound file a meaningful name and a date, so you can find it again.

Carrying out a survey or questionnaire

- Ask participants nicely and thank them afterwards – they are doing you a favour.
- Make sure they understand why you are collecting the data and what you will use it for (unless you have a special situation where this might affect their response). Get permission to use their data, and explain that it will not allow others to identify individual participants' responses if the data are sensitive. Allow participants to withdraw from the study at any point, or to withdraw permission to use their data.
- Make sure that your participants are representative of the population you want to study, and that your sample is not biased towards any particular group which may make the evidence misleading or inaccurate.

2 Project management skills: researching the project

- Ensure that you have enough replies. It is likely that you need at least 30; you may have to ask a lot more than 30 people to respond to your survey to get 30 completed responses.
- Online survey programmes such as Survey Monkey allow your participants to complete the survey online, and help to analyse the data for you.

Analysing and presenting your results

Make sure you allow enough time for sending out the questionnaire, getting responses back and analysing the responses.

How will you record your results? Do you need to summarise your data, for example by calculating mean values? What type of graph (line graph or bar chart) will be most suitable? If it is qualitative data, a graph may be less appropriate.

You could make a graph or chart in a spreadsheet program such as Excel. The same rules for what makes a good graph apply whether you produce it by hand or using software. Make sure you have a title and labels for any axes.

Researchers try to see patterns in their data. Longer answers to open-ended questions may need to be summarised in some way. You can make categories to allow responses to be grouped together, for example, 'people who describe an ice-cream when on holiday', 'people who make their own ice-cream', 'ice-cream linked to another pleasant experience'. This allows you to make semi-quantitative statements such as '45% of people link a particular ice-cream flavour with the people they were with when they first tasted that flavour'. Alternatively, you may just wish to comment on responses, without trying to group or link responses together, or to any pre-determined theory.

Once you have collected and analysed your data, decide what conclusions, if any, can be drawn from your data. How certain can you be of the conclusions (you may relate this for instance to the size of your sample, or the spread of your data)? Should you find out about statistical tests so you can comment more confidently on the certainty of your conclusions? How do your results relate to your research? How will you use the conclusions from your data to inform your project?

> **ACTIVITY Designing and refining survey questions**
>
> You wish to research the link between amount of time spent on social media, and amount of time spent doing homework each week.
>
> Write down one or more research questions. The questions should define the population you are interested in, and the range of channels of social media. Design six questions, and try these out on a sample of 10 people.
>
> Compare your questions and responses with other students in your group. Agree which questions informed the research questions most effectively. What were the characteristics of these questions?
>
> Now redraft the questions in the light of your discussion, and try them out with a different set of students. How did the responses vary? What have you learned about the design of survey questions?

Reading strategies to help you gather relevant information quickly

Skim reading

If we read everything that comes our way in great detail, we would find that time would run out very quickly! We need to be selective and disciplined about the type of reading strategy we use. Skimming allows you to move quickly through the text, look out for key words, data and visuals, and gain an overall idea of the value of the text to your project.

Tips for skim reading:
- read the title, sub titles and any paragraph headings
- look at any visuals, photos and captions
- read the first and last line of every paragraph.

Scanning

Scan reading is about looking for specific information in a document. You would use scanning to find a person's name in a list of entrants in a running race, for example. When scanning in a textbook, you might go straight to the index, then to the relevant page to find the information. Once you've found the information you put down the book and move on.

Detailed study reading

This is where you really need to concentrate to understand the content and meaning of the text. It is a reading strategy commonly used for coursework, project work and when you are preparing for an exam. You are likely to want to take notes.

What this means for my project

When you are taking notes, don't be tempted to copy out long sections. It is not a good use of your time, and will discourage you from using your own words when writing up your report. So, if you think a particular section is of value, write a summary of the main points. A visual representation, such as a diagram, flow chart or table may help. You should also make notes about the source, so you can reference it appropriately in your report and go back to it should you need to. If you want to copy down quotes, make sure you do it using a different colour. You must make it clear if you use direct quotes in your own writing, or this is plagiarism

Key term

Plagiarism is where you use someone else's text or work but give the impression that it is your own work. This is malpractice and must be avoided. For more information on plagiarism, go to page 93.

2 Project management skills: researching the project

ACTIVITY Understanding articles

1 The title has been removed from the following article, so you have lost this clue for what the article is about. First read just the first line of every paragraph in each article. Summarise the article for a partner, or make brief notes.

2 Now read the whole article and decide to what extent you understood the article if you only read the first lines of each paragraph.

> Kirklees Council has been at the forefront in demonstrating the use of renewable energy technology. In order to help reduce carbon emissions it has pioneered the installation of photovoltaic cells and wind turbines to generate electricity on municipal buildings. Local woodlands are harvested to feed woodfuel boilers to reduce carbon emissions; at the same time, this improves woodland habitats for wildlife.
>
> However, the emission savings made by using renewables are minor in the context of what we need to do. This is acknowledged in the national debate about how we move away from fossil fuels to alternative energy sources such as wind, wave and nuclear power. This debate ignores the gross inefficiency of British national housing stock.
>
> A large proportion of houses are poorly insulated so that much of the energy used to heat them is wasted. Within Kirklees a decision has been taken to fund cavity wall and loft insulation for all homes within the district. The principle here is to apply technology appropriately and cost-effectively to deal with energy inefficiency and reduce the demand for energy. This is a much more sustainable approach. The council also aims to ensure that new houses and buildings are built to the highest standards of energy efficiency and have built in renewable energy installations, where possible, over and above that required by central government.
>
> *Based on Learning Skills for Science and reproduced by permission of Gatsby Technical Education Projects*

Key term

Kirklees is a local government district of West Yorkshire in the north of England. Huddersfield is the largest town in the area.

Council The council is a group of people elected to manage the affairs of a city, county or other local government district.

Insulated Temperatures in the UK regularly are below 10 degrees Celsius in the Winter, so people heat their homes. Much of this heat is wasted, if homes are not insulated properly. This insulation is usually material in the walls or roof which prevents the loss of heat.

Recording your research

As you carry out your research, it is vital that you record details of all the sources you have used in your notes. This makes good academic practice for appropriately referencing sources. (If you are using Word, the 'insert references' facility is useful.) Use a grid similar to the one below to record details; this will form a bibliography for your project.

Type of resource: (Book/ Journal article/web page) …

Title: …

Year of publication: …   Place it was published: …

Author(s): …

Are they experts in this field? What are their location, occupation, qualifications? …

Page no. …

For journal articles only: Name of Journal: …

Date of publication: …

For websites only: Date that you accessed the information: …

Published 'Last updated' date: …

Representing information in your own way

When making notes there are a number of techniques you can use which will:
- save you time
- allow you to reproduce ideas and information in your own words
- help you evaluate sources and select information from a variety of sources
- create links and connections between different strands of information and opinion.

ACTIVITY Ways of making notes

1. Think about the techniques you have used successfully in the past for making notes.
2. Discuss your ideas with a partner, if possible, to see if you can gain other suggestions from your peers.

Spidergrams

Look back at page 20 to review how you might use spidergrams to make notes.

Index cards

You can use index cards to summarise the information you collect, or use them to note key words and brief explanations.

2 Project management skills: researching the project

Using tables

Organising information into a table is a good technique when you want to compare categories or record different views or opinions.

Non renewable energy sources	Advantages	Disadvantages
Coal	Large global reserves Widely available	Underground mining is a dangerous activity Public criticism/ environmental damage of modern mining activity
Oil	Ready-made fuel	Supplies more limited than coal Gives off pollutants when burned

ACTIVITY Making notes

1 Choose one technique and take brief notes from the text below

Behaviourists, such as Watson and Skinner, represented the extreme view of environmental determinism. According to them all behaviour is directly shaped and controlled through various types of learning and systems of rewards and punishments. Biologists, on the other hand, adopt the nature side of the debate, and believe that innate biological mechanisms and systems determine our psychological make-up.

Few psychologists now take either of these extreme positions and most would agree that our psychological abilities arise from an interaction between innate and environmental factors. Language ability is a good example to illustrate this interaction: there is now strong evidence that human language acquisition is an innate process. We are 'hard-wired' to speak a language and we possess an inbuilt mechanism that is programmed to recognise grammatical structure. However, the actual language that we speak, e.g. Chinese, English, French, etc., will depend on

the language that we hear spoken around us as we develop. Similarly the range and richness of our vocabulary will largely depend on the models we are presented with. One interesting finding that clearly illustrates how innate and environmental factors affect one another comes from speech perception research in infants. Werker and Tees (1984) showed that infants up to the age of about six months can discriminate between a huge range of sounds found in world languages. However, this ability has disappeared by the time they are about nine months and they seem only to be able to discriminate sounds from the particular language spoken around them. In other words, an external influence, i.e. the language spoken around them, seems to have affected the plasticity of the brain and shaped it to adapt to specific environments.

From Chapter 5 'Perception' by Jane Wilson in the AQA Psychology A A2 Student book. Nelson Thornes 2009

2 Project management skills: researching the project

Using ICT to support your research

> **By the end of this section, you should be able to:**
> ✔ use ICT responsibly
> ✔ understand how some tools of word processing and spreadsheets, and other ICT techniques can help you save time in your research

A computer can help you with your research and writing, but you should consider the health and safety aspects of working at a computer for long periods of time.

Take good care of yourself

It's unlikely, of course, that a computer itself will bring you any real harm, but the regular use of a computer has its hazards. To avoid excessive strain or fatigue, it is worth following these simple guidelines.

Adopt a good posture

Make sure your chair is appropriately adjusted, so you adopt an optimum posture. See the diagram.

Taking good care of yourself

- Learn to touchtype

If you can type with two hands, you will put less strain on your hands and wrists. Learning to touchtype (ie to type with all fingers and thumbs without looking at the keyboard) is even better, since it teaches you the correct positioning of your hands and wrists, and prevents strain from looking up and down between the keyboard and screen.

- Take short, frequent breaks

Taking short breaks will help to avoid RSI (repetitive strain injury), and also relieve your eyes from focusing at a single distance on the computer screen.

- Avoid glare

Adjust your screen so there is no glare caused by sunlight or lighting. Adjust the screen's brightness so that you are looking at it comfortably.

See the previous page too.

Storing and organising your data and files

Your computer hard drive or network area can hold data, information and media files safely until you are ready to use them, or to incorporate them into your report. Consider using an external storage device, like a USB flash drive or external hard drive, to back up your project work. Having a back up procedure is vital to protect all your hard work should anything happen to your computer or laptop. Never just use a flash drive – always have more than one copy. Store information in a form that is accessible on all the computers you use. Keep track of which is the most up-to-date version with dates and even a.m/p.m in the file names.

You may also need to consider the confidential or anonymous nature of the information in your project files. If you have agreed to retain the anonymity of certain subjects, make sure you are honouring this commitment. Keep external drives locked, or ensure that files are password protected.

With the amount of data generated, you will need a simple but effective system of organising and accessing information. Decide on your system for file organisation early on, before the quantity of files and information is difficult to manage. Remember to organise your Bookmarks or Favourites in your web browser too, so you can easily access useful websites.

Useful tools in word processing packages

As well as using a word processing package to write your report, it's worth exploring the other tools these packages can provide.

- **Word count.** There are guidelines to the number of words you should include in your final report. Word can help restrict you to these word limits. Remember that, depending on the version of Word or other word-processing package you have, it won't necessarily count every word.
- **Find and Replace**. If you decide to change your use of a word or phrase or to opt for an alternative spelling, you can use the Find and Replace facility.

2 Project management skills: researching the project

- **Index.** Before structuring and writing your report, you could consider whether or not you intend to use an index. You can generate an index in Word (and insert citations and references). Deciding on which words and phrases to include in an index is an acquired skill in itself. It might be helpful, as a preliminary stage, to create a list of the topics and sub topics you think might appear in your index, then identify the words (entries). When you have identified the entries you want to include, highlight these ready to generate the index. Then follow the instructions in your word-processing software to create the index.
- **Formatting images.** Look for options on formatting images in your word-processor. You can usually fix the image in line with the text (to avoid them 'moving' about as they often do).
- **Template.** Create a template that you can re-use to write letters inviting others to participate in your research. Although email is used for most communications in education and business, a letter of invitation will help your request stand out from a busy email inbox – and help you achieve your objectives. You can also use a template for your report.

What this means for my project

It's important in the early stages of doing your project to take a broad view of the different IT tools available to you so that you can make effective use of them. This will save time and stress in the longer term.

To save time…

- Keyboard shortcuts in word-processing programs help you to use the keyboard in a different way, or to reduce mouse use.

Risk assessment

> **By the end of this section, you should be able to:**
> ✔ carry out a risk assessment relating to the potential risks involved in your project

Students and researchers in higher education institutions often have to carry out risk assessments for their projects. Whilst this might seem natural for a science related project in a chemistry laboratory, it is actually widespread across all subject areas. Employers have a legal requirement to carry out risk assessments in the workplace in order to protect the health and safety of their employees. Your risk assessment will help you understand the appropriate use of any safety equipment, and what you need to do in order to avoid any risk to your own health and safety.

What this means for my project

Even if you are developing a line of work which doesn't seem hazardous, for example, in the social sciences or related to MFL (modern foreign languages), you are still required to carry out a risk assessment. If your project involves other people, or meeting external experts, for example, there may be health and safety aspects you need to consider. If your project involves a topic area new to you, you may need to consider unfamiliar skills or techniques.

There are six key steps you need to consider when carrying out a risk assessment for your project.

1. Look out for hazards and the potential for harm.
2. Be aware of who your project might affect and possibly harm.
3. Decide on the severity and likelihood of the risks, and what you could do to prevent them.
4. Review your risk assessment and revise it if necessary.
5. Having implemented your risk reductions, discuss your risk assessment with your Project Supervisor.
6. Remember to monitor, amend and update your project plan in line with your risk assessment.

For more information on the health & safety issues in your particular subject discipline, talk to your Project Supervisor.

Drawing up a risk assessment grid

It is worth drawing up a grid to help organise your risk assessment. The criteria in the grid will trigger your thoughts about different risks, including their severity and likelihood.

Risk Assessment grid							
Name:				Project title:			
	Severity of risk: what is the possible impact?			Likelihood of risk			Overall risk
Risk type	High	Medium	Low	High	Medium	Low	
Legal							
Financial							
Personal health & safety							
Health & safety of others							
Confidentiality of others							
Relying on resources							
Personal reputation							
Other:							
Detail the steps you will take to minimise the risks 1 2 3							

ACTIVITY Risk assessment

1. Carry out a risk assessment of your project.
2. Discuss your risk assessment with your Project Supervisor

Skills to help your project run smoothly

> **By the end of this section, you should be able to:**
> ✔ understand the value of applying critical thinking and analytical skills to your project research and development
> ✔ identify how decision making and problem solving skills can help you make good decisions more effectively
> ✔ apply creative thinking skills to your project to help you manage obstacles.

What do we mean by critical thinking?

Critical thinkers take nothing they read or see for granted. Useful for advanced level and undergraduate work, critical thinking skills require you to:

- refer to the model or criteria you are going to evaluate against (such as the status of the author of a journal article)
- carry out a careful and detailed evaluation of resources and materials used in your research, checking they are appropriate and up to date
- evaluate the evidence for any claims made by the author
- look for any potential bias
- weigh up all opinions and arguments so your discussion is supported through reasoning.

These are the main elements that make up critical thinking relating to research. These skills apply to a variety of subject areas and professions (imagine lawyers, engineers, or journalists without critical and analytical thinking).

Critical thinking skills are also valuable in daily life. Consider English Premier League Football where managers are easily dismissed as soon as their team fails to win a few games. One argument regularly put forward is that teams need a stable, long-standing manager in order to succeed (teams like Manchester United and Arsenal are often quoted to 'substantiate' this). But should this logic necessarily be taken at face value? What this argument fails to acknowledge is that these managers are often stable because of success, not the other way around.

2 Project management skills: researching the project

Seeing the whole picture

It's only when you see the whole picture, you know what is really going on.

Statistics may only tell part of the story

ACTIVITY Evaluating statistics

This table is from a Royal Academy of Engineering publication *The Cost of Generating Electricity*. Cost is an important factor when making decisions about energy policy. Consider the table below which shows the costs of electricity generation from different sources.

Source	Cost in p / kW hour
Gas-fired Combined Cycle Gas Turbine (CCGT)	2. 2
Nuclear fission plant	2. 3
Coal-fired pulverised-fuel (PF) steam plant	2. 5
Coal-fired circulating fluidised bed (CFB) steam plant	2. 6
Coal-fired integrated gasification combined cycle (IGCC)	3. 2
Poultry litter-fired bubbling fluidised bed	6. 8
Onshore wind farm	3. 7
Offshore wind farm	5. 5
Wave and marine technologies	6. 6

1. Do these costs give us the full picture? Research the 'hidden' costs of nuclear power. In a search engine, type in 'cost of nuclear'.
2. Write down additional costs involved in producing electricity from nuclear fission.
3. What other 'costs' might be involved in producing electricity, other than economic costs?

Based on Learning Skills for Science and reproduced by permission of Gatsby Technical Education Projects.

Statistics: strengths and weaknesses

What do statistics tell you?

Scientists and social scientists are often interested in describing real-life phenomena, such as the economic market, sales, examination performance, or behaviour of students in school. They do this by collecting data, then using these data to make conclusions.

It is important to have some knowledge and understanding of statistics if you wish to use data to support your own ideas. You also need this to be critically aware of others' use of statistics.

You have probably used graphs and bar charts to present data. Being able to describe data and use it to make inferences are useful additional skills.

Sampling and descriptive statistics

Researchers are often interested in findings that apply to whole populations. It is not normally possible to collect data from every individual in a population, so data is collected from a manageable sample of the population of interest.

'Populations' and 'samples': if you were interested in the sports played by male 16–18 students, your population is male students of 16–18 years old. You use the results from your sample to infer things about the whole population of male 16–18 year old students. In order to do this, your sample size must be large enough to include most of the variation present within the population. The sample must be representative of the population, that is, not biased. If you only looked at students from private international schools, your sample would be biased.

The mean of a set of values is often used to describe the data. Measures of how spread out the data are (such as standard deviation) are also important. Measures of the spread of the data are often shown as 'error bars' on graphs, and these should be taken into account when describing trends in data

Large sample size is important. Otherwise the mean of your sample may not represent the mean of the whole population. If you take a number of large, random samples from a population, you would not expect the mean to vary very much.

If you counted the games of football (soccer) played by 16-18 year old male students in schools in two very different cities, you may find two different mean values. Depending on how different these means are, it may not be possible to tell wither this difference suggests these are two different populations (eg 16-18 year old male students playing football in a school with a very strong, active football club or 16-18 year old male students playing football in a school without a football club) or whether the difference you have observed is normal variation due to chance. You may need to perform a statistical test to determine whether this difference is statistically significant.

Be critical of data

A customer satisfaction survey that asks people to rate a product 1–5 will show a different result depending on how the data is clumped. If a bar chart is drawn with only three groups (good satisfaction, medium satisfaction and low satisfaction) this could mask the fact that no- one has rated the product 5.

A claim that young mothers are less likely to take exercise than other groups was based on a sample of young mothers in a mother and baby group. Was this sample representative of all young mothers? Is any bias in the sampling likely to affect the results?

Here are some tips to help ensure that you can rely on the numbers.

1. Be clear about what you want to discover when you collect your data.
2. Make sure any assertions are backed up by evidence, and your report is not claiming causation when this is not proven.
3. Make sure that your samples are from your chosen population.
4. Ensure that your sample size is large enough . Your sample must also be random within your population, without bias to any particular group within it.
5. Some claims rely heavily on the mean of a data sample, but you should look at the spread of the data too.
6. Claims are more valid if the same study has been repeated with similar results.

What this means for my project

Remember that facts and figures may only tell half of the story. You will develop your critical thinking skills throughout your post-16 studies, and your IPQ will help. Like most skills, they improve with practice.

Assessment criteria for the IPQ require you to use critical thinking when evaluating resources and information as part of your project. In the same way, the approach you use to review others' writing, information, and evidence during your research should be applied to your own report writing. So, for example, when you quote a particular reference or source, you must be sure that it really does back up what you are saying.

Key term

Critical thinking Also known as analytical thinking, it is a process used to analyse and evaluate information and arguments.

2 Project management skills: researching the project

Decision making and problem solving skills

Poor decision making will hold up progress on your project, and use up precious time. Some people find decision making comes more naturally to them than others. However most students could focus on improving the quality of their decision making skills in order to make good judgements.

Decision making and problem solving are closely linked, since problem solving often needs you to evaluate and select from a range of alternative options. Problem solving can be applied to a variety of different situations; you can apply these skills to any task, activity, or decision related to your project – or events and issues in your personal life.

The process of decision making can usually be broken down into a number of straightforward steps.

1. Does a decision need to be made? What will be the impact if I don't make a decision?
2. Is the issue/task urgent or important, or possibly both?
3. What exactly is the main issue or cause of the problem? What type of problem is it? How have I solved similar problems in the past?
4. Draw up a list of all the possible options and solutions along with their pros and cons (advantages and disadvantages) (see section on 'generating ideas' on page 21).

   'In any moment of decision, the best thing you can do is the right thing, the next best thing is the wrong thing, and the worst thing you can do is nothing.' (Attributed to Theodore Roosevelt)

> **Study tip**
>
> Don't forget to keep your Project Supervisor up to date with your progress.
>
> If you find yourself stuck and unable to progress effectively, discuss this with your Supervisor. Your Supervisor can be a good source of advice and guidance, even if you feel you're making good progress.

2 Project management skills: researching the project

ACTIVITY Decision making

Imagine you are having to make a tough decision, for example, whether to do some charity/voluntary work, or buying a second hand car. Draw up a list of pros and cons for your decision.

Should I do regular voluntary work one evening a week whilst continuing with my studies?	
Pros (all those arguments for this decision; the advantages)	Cons (all those arguments against this decision; the disadvantages)
Total . . . pros	Total …. cons

Expanding the pros and cons decision making process

You can expand the pros and cons technique to weight your pros and cons. This allows you to take into account that not all disadvantages will carry the same weight or have the same impact. In the example above, you might think that being able to describe volunteering experience on your personal statement/or resume/CV is worth more than the enjoyment you will get from the experience, for example. These weightings are entirely subjective – there is no right or wrong argument. The criteria will depend on your own personal set of preferences which may change over time, with your situation, or even with your mood.

You can use whatever scoring method you want to: you can score with 1-5 points, or an A, B, C scoring method or even award 10, 20 or 100 stars. It's entirely up to you.

The weightings may recommend you take a decision that you feel uncomfortable with. If so, you may need to look again at how you weighted different factors, or whether you missed out some significant arguments on either side.

With this sort of technique, you can add anything to either column that you think relates to your decision. This might also include emotional issues such as 'I'll feel more confident' or 'It will be a load off my mind'. At the same time, by listing and measuring options, it allows you to be more objective.

See the activity overleaf

2 Project management skills: researching the project

ACTIVITY Scoring pros and cons

1 Using the pros and cons you listed on the previous page, apply your own scoring method to weight the different elements.

Should I do regular voluntary work on evening a week whilst continuing with my studies?			
Pros (all those arguments for this decision; the advantages)	**Weighting score**	**Cons** (all those arguments against this decision; the disadvantages)	**Weighting score**
Total . . . pros		Total …. cons	

2 How did the weighting scores affect your final decision?

SWOT analysis decision making process

SWOT analysis can be applied to help structure any decision making process. It forces you to consider issues that you may otherwise avoid in an instinctive, emotional response. It is regularly used in business to assess decisions such as 'Is this new business idea viable?' or 'Should we enter into this strategic partnership?'

A SWOT analysis would usually be presented in grid form with four squares, one for each of:

S: Strengths

W: Weaknesses (usually related to internal factors)

O: Opportunities

T: Threats (usually related to external factors; the outside world)

Strengths	Weaknesses
What are the advantages of this proposition? What are our strengths (such as people, assets, resources, IT, communications)?	What are the disadvantages? What are the gaps in our knowledge, capability, and so on? What would make us vulnerable?
Opportunities	**Threats**
What's going on in the world that would actually make this a positive outcome? What are the trends that we can capitalise on?	What are the external factors that would have a negative impact on us? What are the external factors that would create obstacles?

ACTIVITY SWOT analysis

1 Consider a decision you have to make about how to carry out part of your project.

2 Carry out a SWOT analysis to help you with your decision.

Creative thinking

Creative thinking uses less controlled and less predictable approaches to problem solving and decision making. The approaches could lead to some new ideas, but can often involve some risk-taking. Creative thinking is where:

- you look for a combination of answers rather than one
- you allow yourself to play with ideas, and to make any number of crazy suggestions which may or may not be 'right'
- you learn from what went well, but learn even more from the mistakes or extreme ideas you put forward.

Here are some ways of encouraging your creative thinking.

- Play with a puzzle or toy requiring you to use your hands: some people find that stimulating the tips of your fingers activates nerves in the brain, and this gets you thinking differently.
- Go for a walk along a different route. This allows your mind to work over an idea.
- Put on a type of music that you might not normally listen to.
- Do some things differently for a day, whether it's trying a new food or having a conversation with someone at school you've not spoken to before.
- Try to come up with 15 different answers to the same question. Generate more answers by saying 'If I were in high spirits, my answer would be … '; 'If I were grumpy, my answer would be …'; and so on.

In fact, ideas can flow at any time – sometimes when you least expect them. Remember to note them down on your phone or in a notebook so that they don't get forgotten.

2 Project management skills: researching the project

ACTIVITY Creative thinking

1 Select a situation from those listed below, and apply one of the techniques described above (or combine more than one), to arrive at a 'solution' or answer.

A None of the people you invite to take part in your research accept, but time is running out.

B Materials you'd planned to use prove difficult to get hold of within your deadline; your Supervisor suggests you research an alternative, but you are unsure.

C An experiment you planned as part of your research does not go well, but you are not sure why.

What this means for my project

It is likely that at some point your project will hit an obstacle. This is not unusual. In fact, you need some obstacles to produce a good IPQ Production Log! You can apply some of the skills practised in this section to overcome any problems and decide on your next action. As part of your IPQ, you will need to describe how and why you arrived at each solution and describe any changes. Keep a record of:

_ what the problem involved, and its potential impact on your project (in terms of time, money, the scope of your project, and so on)

_ the options and solutions you considered, along with their advantages and disadvantages

_ how you arrived at your solution

_ the impact of your solution

_ your evaluation of the situation. For example, how well did your solution work? What else would you have done differently?

> **Study tip**
>
> Don't forget to keep your Supervisor up to date with what you are doing. They might have helpful advice or questions you've simply not thought of. They also need to have a good idea of what you are doing for your final assessment.

Your mid-term review

> **By the end of this section, you should be able to:**
> ✔ understand the purpose of the mid-term review meeting, and how it helps you develop your project
> ✔ identify the most appropriate format for your report
> ✔ What your mid-term review is for

It is normal practice for your Project Supervisor to conduct a mid-term review meeting with each student involved in an Independent Project. Your Supervisor will decide with you the appropriate time to hold this discussion. This is likely to be when you have completed most of your research and preparatory work, and are ready to start writing your report.

It is up to you to complete page 13 of the Oxford AQA Exams Candidate Record Form, Production Log & Assessment Record. You may complete this during or after the meeting; you could make some notes on a draft copy of the form during the meeting and then write them up in full afterwards on the final form.

The purpose of the mid-term review meeting is to have a full discussion of what you have done so far, so that your Supervisor can:

- support and help you to decide on your final project evidence
- assess your progress so far in full.

What this meeting means in practice is that you will be able to:

- highlight any issues that might have arisen so far, and discuss any changes to your original project plan
- review your risk assessment and the precautions you are taking
- examine the best route forward, taking into account any problems and successes you've experienced so far.

Remember the Oxford AQA Exams IPQ Assessment Objectives

Remind yourself of the relevant Assessment Objectives. Use your mid-term review to check you are on track to achieve your best grade.

At this point, the relevant criteria are:

Assessment Objective[2]	Grading Criteria
AO2 **Planning, monitoring and developing** • Produce a project plan which includes a schedule detailing the tasks you will do and when you will do them • Carry out a risk assessment to assess the health, safety, and risk issues associated with your project • Monitor your progress against the objectives you set yourself	Grade A 'There is comprehensive monitoring of progress against the plan, and the selection of a monitoring technique is clearly justified.' 'Project development is detailed, clear and justified throughout.' *In other words:* Your research at this point may have given you huge amounts of information and data. You must now select the most appropriate information for your project title. If necessary, you may need to refine the focus of your project and redraft the title, in order to keep to the required word limit and your schedule.
AO3 **Demonstration of research skills** • Research a range of different information and resources appropriate to your research • Select the most appropriate resources for you to use • Examine the resources critically • Organise the information and resources you gather • Justify the selection of any secondary and primary resources you use	'Sources are selected for a clear and justified purpose and relevant information from them is identified systematically and effectively. Sources are subjected to scrutiny to assess their validity.' *In other words:* You need to make sure you select the most relevant resources and make clear how you have assessed if they are valid, and that you can justify their use as evidence in your report. You should always remember to reference the sources of your research and be very organised in how you record your research.

[2]© Oxford AQA Exams 2017 Please refer to the current version of the specification on the Oxford AQA Exams website at www.oxfordaqaexams.org.uk/subjects/projects/ipq

2 Project management skills: researching the project

Assessment Objective[2]	Grading Criteria
AO4 **Analysis and application of research** - Implement the project plan - Analyse the findings of the project research - Arrange these findings in a 5000 word report - Include a conclusion to your report and communicate your outcomes - Include a bibliography and references and any other appropriate appendices to your report *(This highlights the most relevant aspects of the Assessment Objective at this stage in your project; for a full account of all AOs, see page 40)*	'The project plan is implemented clearly throughout.' *In other words:* You need to make sure that you implement the original project plan. If changes are needed to your project plan (or your aims and objective), make sure you provide clear reasons and explanations for these changes. Record any techniques you used in order to overcome problems and arrive at decisions. Making mistakes or changing course can be positive. Just make sure you keep a record of the decision processes you used when making changes to your plan. 'The report is of appropriate length and writing style, with a clear focus on the final title throughout. The project is organised well and referenced appropriately.' *In other words:* Remember you are limited by time and the number of words that you can write in your report. At this point you can review your progress against your time and the word limit. Do you still think you can achieve your objectives within the time available? Is it likely your report will be within the word limit guidelines. If your answer is 'No' to either of these questions, then you need to make changes so that you can still meet the Assessment Objectives. Work out what gaps there are in your research and what still needs to be done in order to lead to an appropriate conclusion in your report, and that your report meets the requirements. (For example, have you got all the information you need to put together a bibliography?)

Examples of students' work

Here are extracts from real examples of the mid-term review from previous students' Candidate Record Form, Production Log & Assessment Record, reproduced by permission of Oxford AQA Exams. You could discuss how well you think these students are doing.

Warning – these samples of work from pilot candidates may reflect earlier versions of the specification and/or required documentation. However, they demonstrate the ways in which a project plan might develop and change at the mid-term review stage.

Project title:
A pastiche of a James Joyce short story based on a stylistic analysis of Dubliners

Outline the successes, failures, additions and/or changes you made as you followed your plan at start of project

When reading the novels I realised that … I was presented with three obvious options regarding the style I would adopt – I could imitate the 'stream of consciousness' in Ulysses, the development of language with age in Portrait of the Artist, or I could write a missing story from Dubliners. I chose to do the latter – and so began research into Dubliners. The state of Dublin is, obviously, a very important topic in Dubliners – as the stories focus on the lives of everyday, unremarkable people, living their lives in the city of Dublin. So I realised that the small amount of knowledge I had on Dublin needed to be expanded if I was going to write about it. …. I decided that rather than write the missing story in Dubliners I would update it, and write a story imitating Joyce's style, but about life in Bolton, in the 21st century. … Once I had decided this I researched Joyce's background and his attitude to issues with my own background and attitude in mind, trying to draw parallels between the state of society today and the state of society in Dublin when Joyce was writing. Looking at the technical side of his writing did not pose a problem as it could still be imitated – and although I have found that most themes can be translated to modern times there are some that are redundant – such as the union of Ireland with Britain – and some new issues that can be discussed.

Outline your planned steps to complete your project

I have read the introduction to Dubliners, and a critical work on Joyce … I have made notes on all I deemed relevant to my research. … I will read through my notes and make a general list of all techniques and issues which I will imitate in my writing, which I will refer to during my writing … After having come to a conclusion I will make a plan for my story – and begin to write it. Once my story is written I will then compare my own writing with the notes I have made during my research on Joyce's own writing and write an analysis accordingly.

Project title:

Given the rapid development and ever increasing funding for nanotechnology, and questions about its safe use, is it ethically right that it is so widely used by commerce and industry?

Outline the successes, failures, additions and/or changes you made as you followed your plan at the start of project

The main alteration that I have decided to make upon starting my project is to take out my section focused on the funding of research of nanotechnology at universities, as well as the funding of other scientific research. … Specific information has been very difficult to come by, as I have tried looking in published documents and books, using the internet, and even a professor specialising in nanotechnology…. The professor seemed to be particularly reluctant to share information regarding the funding of the research carried out. …

Your Supervisor's main comments and advice at this stage

I have been told by my supervisor that my essay is coming together well, but I must concentrate on citing my work properly. … As a result of discussion with my Supervisor I have decided to bring another area into my dissertation. I would like to investigate the reasons that information about funding has been so difficult to come across ….

Changes, clarifications or additions you have made as a result of your discussion with your Supervisor at this stage

I have revised my methods of citing within my project, utilising the Harvard System … The main problem with my work before this alteration was that I had consulted a wide range of sources in doing my research, and I had brought them all together to form my own opinions, which I then wrote in my essay, leading to a messy job in citing all these sources. I have now better arranged my ideas …

Project title

In areas of clinical practice, how successful have attempts been to combat the threat posed by viral Hepatitis B?

Your supervisor's main comments and advice at this stage

As we feared earlier I have got too much research and information, and my Supervisor has now advised me to stop any further research as I have too much of it and it will take a lot longer than we anticipated to edit my essay to fit the allowed word count.

Changes, clarifications or additions you have made as a result of your discussion with your Supervisor at this stage

I still want to include in my essay information that will allow the reader to fully understand my study, and this is impossible without including all the basic information. I understand the editing process will take a long time and that I will have to take large sections out of my current essay once it is finished ….

2 Project management skills: researching the project

Planning your project product (written report)

The format of your report may depend on what is appropriate to the topic or task undertaken for your project. It will be useful to discuss this at your mid-term review. The format will be:

- a written report of approximately 5000 words

Your report will be about 5000 words in length; you are allowed +/-10% allowance on this. This means your report should be more than 4500 words, but less than 5500 words in length.

This word limit should not include:

- the bibliography
- any description of sources or how you have validated them
- or any reasons you have for selecting the sources.
- blank questionnaires (if you have used them) to include as an example in the appendices.

You must choose an appropriate writing style for your report, but it is likely you will want it to be formal and academic in style. A science-based essay may be different to a humanities essay; each of them will have a slightly different style, format, and 'voice'. There is no accepted or recommended template or expected format. It is up to you to decide what is most appropriate for the subject content of your research.

Consider how you will structure your report, and the style of writing of your report. Discuss your options with your Supervisor at the mid-term project review meeting.

> **Study tip** Students achieving good results were those who had thought through the appropriate form of their report with Supervisor guidance.

Checklist – are you ready for your mid-term review?

As part of the assessment evidence for your independent project, you are required to discuss your project with your Supervisor at a mid-term review meeting. This stage is critical in the journey of your IPQ, and if necessary, allows you to re-set your sights and establish the most appropriate format for your project report. Your Supervisor will be very willing to support you through this review process, but will be more able to help you effectively if you have prepared for the meeting.

Use this checklist to make sure you're appropriately prepared for meeting your Supervisor[3].

	Your notes
I have evaluated the resources I found, to establish those most relevant to my project by …	
The way I identified the most reliable sources was …	
The range of resources that I have consulted appropriate to my project title include the following types of media …	
My preferred technique for note-taking to record my references is …	
My preferred technique for note-taking to record useful information and add my own ideas is …	
The best way I can make use of ICT to support my research is …	
According to my risk assessment, the overall risks in my project are …	
I have taken the following precautions …	
Examples of where I have applied the principles of critical thinking include …	
Where I have used techniques of decision making, problem solving and creative thinking I have recorded these in the following way: …	
The questions I want to ask my Supervisor at my mid-term review meeting are:	
What else do I need to do?	

---

[3] Filling in this chart is not an Oxford AQA Exams requirement for your IPQ. However it may help you to prepare for a meeting with your Supervisor.

Project progress checkpoint

▶ **1 Project management skills: starting out**

▼ **2 Project management skills: researching the project**

Have you discussed your project at a mid-term review meeting?	Yes	No
Have you completed page 13 of your Candidate Record Form, Production Log & Assessment Record?	Yes	No
Have you considered and finalised the format for your written report?	Yes	No

▶ **3 Project management skills: producing the project report**

▶ **4 Presenting your project**

▶ **5 Finalising and submitting your project**

▶▶▶ **Next steps**

The next stage of your Independent Project Qualification will be to write your report.
▶▶▶

Project management skills: producing the project product

3

As a result of the discussion and advice gained in your mid-term review meeting, you should review your original plan. Make any necessary adjustments to your plan, keeping in mind the IPQ Assessment Objectives, and the need to work within the boundaries of time and word length.

This chapter focuses on the development of your project's report and your academic writing skills. The skills developed here are likely to be useful to all students, whatever the subject area of your project.

This chapter will help you to:
- ✔ select the best presentation style for your report
- ✔ examine different styles of writing and develop your own report writing skills
- ✔ use the accepted format for referencing sources in your report
- ✔ apply planning and time management skills to your project product
- ✔ prepare for your project product review meeting.

'Now where exactly did I find that quote?'

3 Project management skills: producing the project product

Report writing skills

> **By the end of this section, you should be able to:**
> ✔ distinguish between the different models of report writing, and select the best structure for your report
> ✔ select an appropriate writing style for your subject matter
> ✔ acknowledge the different stages in the writing process and the benefits of re- writing your first draft
> ✔ define the overall structure for your report, and the elements the report is likely to include.

Part of the assessment evidence required for your Independent Project is a written report of 5000 words. The report should also include appendices (such as a bibliography and references), but any other appendices you include will depend on the topic and subject chosen. Bibliography and appendices do not contribute to your word count.

Selecting the presentation style of your report

You should aim to write a report of an appropriate length (ie more than 4500 words, but less than 5500), and written in an appropriate style. The report should respond to your topic with well-argued, referenced research. You must communicate clearly, but in a style which is appropriate for your subject matter. The quality of your communication skills is partly reflected in the presentation style that you adopt for your report. Once you have chosen the format for the report, it is important to stick to this and to the word limits specified. This reflects the requirements of universities and employers, where many publications, journals or companies ask that articles or reports are submitted in a particular format and length.

A written report

For the IPQ, your written report should be approximately 5000 words. This might be an investigation, exploration of a hypothesis, extended essay or academic report.

> **Study tip**
> It is important to keep within the word limits. Many students have felt frustrated when their reports have been too long. This often relates to inappropriate planning of the report and a lack of clear focus when writing starts.

3 Project management skills: producing the project product

You will have come across a range of reports during your education, and may have met many different styles of writing in your project research. Academic journals lay down their own requirements for style, length and format. You could look online, for example, at:

- Oxford Journals, published by Oxford University Press, and search for 'Instructions to Authors'
- Elsevier, who also publish journals, and their 'Guide for Authors'

Here are some samples of different types of reports and writing styles.

From 'History Today', – see their website.

A Woman at Waterloo

Andrew Roberts introduces the remarkable memoir of Magdalene De Lancey, wife of Wellington's chief of staff, who accompanied her husband on a campaign that climaxed in triumph and tragedy.

Reproduced by permission of History Today.

From Catalyst magazine – see the Catalyst website from SEP

'Tree power' by Janet Taylor

Humans have been using the warmth and light from wood fires for hundreds of thousands of years. Even now up to half the people in the world cook their food on open fires. Wood fuel is in the news again now because it is a renewable source of energy. At present almost all our energy in Britain comes from fossil fuels and in the long run these will run out.

Burning fossil fuels also releases carbon dioxide and contributes to global climate change. We need to replace them with renewable and more sustainable sources of power.

Reproduced by permission of Gatsby Technical Education Projects

---

From The Times online (TLS)

Shakespeare and deep England: Jonathan Bate's eloquent evocation of the man from Warwickshire

John Guy writes: 'At last we have a new kind of biography of Shakespeare. Starting from Ben Jonson's description of Shakespeare as "Soul of the Age", and shunning "the

deadening march of chronological sequence that is biography's besetting vice", Jonathan Bate selects only the material that, he believes, will help to reveal Shakespeare's cultural DNA.'

Reproduced by permission of The Times Literary Supplement, www.the-tls.co.uk

3 Project management skills: producing the project product

From Business Review, Philip Allen Updates

Extract from 'The credit crunch' by Ian Marcousé

The reward structure

Both in the USA and in Britain, investment banks encouraged staff to look for innovative ways to achieve profitable deals. Some were offered a bonus per deal; most received a bonus each year based on the profits their deals achieved. These bonuses might amount to £1 million or more per person. The individual could pocket that sum, knowing that even if the deal went sour a year later, the bonus could not be clawed back. It was a classic 'Heads I win, tails you lose' situation. What's more, the individual with the biggest bonus would probably also be identified as the best candidate for promotion, to encourage the others. Therefore, the logical approach for ambitious bank executives was to maximise their bonus-yielding 'profits'.

Reproduced by permission of Philip Allen Updates.

ACTIVITY Different writing styles

1. Look at the examples of articles above and on the previous page. Collect up a range of magazines and journals relevant to your IPQ topic area from your school library or the Internet. Select a range of articles and reports. Consider their style by carrying out a review, using these questions to guide you.

    A   Is there an abstract? What role does it play?

    B   Is there an introduction? What is its length compared with the whole article or report?

    C   Does the report refer to a specific piece of research? What were the methods and materials used?

    D   How are any findings described?

    E   How does the discussion unfold? Is more than one point of view put forward?

    F   When and how are the conclusions explained?

    G   What illustrations or photos are included? What do the visuals add to the work

2. A   Which style is most appropriate for the field of your own research?

    B   Create a template in Word or another word-processing package which reflects the format you feel is most appropriate to your subject area. Save the template so you can use or adapt it in future.

    C   Agree with your Supervisor to send your work to them electronically so they can check your template.

3 Project management skills: producing the project product

Using visuals in your report

Imagine a world with no visuals. How much time do we waste by using words instead of pictures? It is worth considering the role of illustrations, photos, and other images in communicating or reinforcing ideas in your report.

> **ACTIVITY Interpreting visuals**
>
> **1** Work with a partner, and with some visuals related to ideas or processes relevant to your projects. Partner A describes a visual which Partner B has not seen. Partner A has two minutes to describe the ideas or processes being portrayed, rather than the visual itself. Meanwhile Partner B draws the picture from the description.
>
> **2** At the end of two minutes, Partner B shows their picture to Partner A. Discuss how difficult or easy it was to interpret what was being said. How similar/different are the drawings to the original? Was it difficult to communicate the ideas from the drawing? Partners A and B swap roles and repeat the process using another visual.
>
> Activity based on Learning Skills for Science and reproduced by permission of Gatsby Technical Education Projects

Processing and representing data

Just as an image can enhance a piece of text and make it more accessible to a reader, graphs can quickly summarise and present large amounts of data – making the data easier to understand.

> **Study tip**
>
> Remember that if you do use images in your report you must acknowledge sources for them. All images, tables, graphs, etc., that you use (even if these are your own) must have a reference for where you found them.

> **Key term**
>
> **An abstract** is a very brief summary of the content of your report.

3 Project management skills: producing the project product

ACTIVITY Journal article analysis

1 Read the extracts below (or longer articles), and use this grid to help you consider the features of the language used.

Features/language style	Comments
Is the 'passive' (the IPQ book was placed on the table) or 'active' voice (she put the IPQ book on the table) more likely to be used?	
Are the articles written in the first person ('I did …'), second person ('you did …') or third person ('he/she/it did …')?	
In what circumstances is the past tense used?	
When might it be more appropriate to use the present tense?	
Do report writers use emotional language or objective, impersonal language?	
Do the writers make use of colloquial words or phrases?	

Article from *Gramophone*

Curtain rises on La Scala season amid dramas offstage

The annual December 7 opening night of the season at La Scala is traditionally a high-profile event but in recent years it has become just as well known for the dramas behind the scenes. Sure enough, as applause and occasional booing greeted the new production of Verdi's Don Carlo, *… tempers had barely cooled after a dispute over pay for musicians and staff.*

Reproduced by permission of Gramophone

Article from *Catalyst*, April 2006

Venus Express by David Sang

The Venus Express spacecraft was launched at 3.30 in the morning on 9 November…. The trip to Venus lasts 153 days. For most of this time, the strongest force on the craft is the pull of the Sun's gravity. Once Venus Express is captured by Venus's own gravitational pull, the engineers at the control centre in Darmstadt, Germany, need 5 days to manoeuvre it into its operational orbit. There is no lander on this craft; it is planned to follow an extended elliptical path around the planet. This takes it first within 250 km

of the planet's surface, and then far out, 66 000 km into space, before it plunges back inwards once more.

Reproduced by permission of Gatsby Technical Education Projects

Spas: How toxic is your 'natural' spa? by Erin Gill, *Daily Telegraph*, November 2008

Everyone loves being pampered but are the ingredients as pure as you think?

Before you let your mind switch off, there is one niggling worry that might be worth investigating. What goes into all those body wraps, scrubs, lifts and refreshers? Is that facial made from 100 per cent fresh papaya or are there other less natural ingredients in it too? The short answer to that question is yes. In many cases the products used during spa treatments are not nearly as natural as all those references to algae and rose essence imply. Depending on what the products are designed to achieve, they may include detergents, synthetic fragrance, a range of preservatives ... the list goes on.

© Daily Telegraph Media Group Limited 2008

Extract from *The Hub*, London College of Fashion, May 2008

Future research

A key concept for Fashion Science is fashion as a vehicle to deliver greater functionality, satisfaction and delight to wearers across the broad spectrum of clothing and accessories for personal health and wellbeing, sportswear, casual clothing and high fashion. The challenge is to balance the drive for constant change and renewal, with its resulting obsolescence, against the industry's global economic importance in sustaining trade, employment and livelihoods. Some of the questions the Centre for Fashion Science will tackle include: Can consumers be persuaded to buy less but cleverer clothes and can consumption be reduced through intelligent application of science and technology to enhance fashion design and production?

Reproduced by permission of Professor Sandy Black, London College of Fashion

3 Project management skills: producing the project product

Think about the language of your report

Classic features of academic writing

As well as bearing the audience in mind, academic writing has a number of typical features:
- It is formal rather than informal.
- It does not usually include colloquial words and phrases.
- The author writes in complete sentences.
- It is written objectively, so that the reader can understand what has been researched and studied rather than what the writer 'believes'.
- The writer is accountable for what they say, and can provide evidence or an argument for their ideas.
- It avoids sexist language and stereotypes, such as referring to a professor or judge automatically as 'he'
- It is precise, using language efficiently and effectively (no redundant, vague, or long-winded language).

ACTIVITY Writing styles

1 Bearing in mind what you have learned from your analysis of the articles and from reading about the features of academic writing, decide which of the following versions of the phrases in the table would be more appropriate to your report. Both are acceptable – which do you prefer?

A	Several possibilities surfaced …		Several possibilities occurred to us	
B	This paper examines		We examined	
C	I hope		It is hoped	
D	It is suggested that …		This is…	
E	You can easily forget		It is easy to forget	
F	The data indicates		I saw from the data that ….	
G	This suggests		The evidence suggests	
H	XXX asserts …		XXX says ….	

2 The following words and phrases are considered to be informal and colloquial. Identify alternatives which would be more appropriate to your academic report.
- Stuff
- Lots of
- Sort of
- Go down (the shops)
- Lab
- Nice
- OK
- Again and again

Manage the writing process

Plan your report or essay

Work out the overall structure in terms of the paragraphs or sections. Refer to your 'ideas shower' notes. Produce headings and sub headings for the entire report.

Make notes under each sub-heading to say what it will include, how it addresses the question or hypothesis in your project title, and how it links with the previous and following sections.

List the research findings and sources you will refer to under each sub-heading. Make a note of how these will relate to the project question or hypothesis.

As well as thinking about what to include, think about what you should be leaving out. Work out roughly how many words each section should have in order to achieve the overall word allowances for your report.

Also work out how much time you can afford to give to each section in order to keep to your schedule.

Write down all sorts of ideas for the different parts of your report

Write down the key ideas that have emerged in your argument. Create sub-topics to each of these main ideas. This stage helps a great deal in organising your own thoughts. It should also give you confidence, as you set out exactly what you have achieved so far.

Draw up your conclusion first

This is an accepted part of academic writing and although it appears illogical, it's not. You have to know where you'll end up when you embark on a writing journey. It also helps create a more coherent report, with earlier sections leading logically to your ending.

Your conclusion should aim to summarise the 'answer' to your research and draw together the main points of your argument. It is not a place to introduce new ideas, but should bring an authoritative closure to your report.

Get writing – anything!

At this stage, it's important just to start writing. This will be your first draft, so don't worry too much about the accuracy or the flow of your sentences. It's the overall ideas you need to get on screen first.

Reference your sources as you write

Use the citations you stored at the research stage. It is very time consuming to try and put references in when the report is finished.

Rigorously edit and cut

This is where you go over your first draft and improve it. This re-drafting will be far more effective if you've allowed a few days between writing and re-writing. Go back to the structure you drew up, and make sure your report is following this. Use powerful language not clichés; vary the phrases you use to convince your reader; and carefully review the language you use for arguing a point of view.

What do you think of the next paragraph? See the activity on page 92.

Keep sentences short because it is easy to lose track of an argument in long sentences which have lots of clauses and sub-clauses and which are divided up by a large number of commas, which are supposed to break up the sense of the sentence, but which actually add to the confusion, by introducing new ideas, cluttering your brain and preventing the main point of the argument from coming over. Read your writing aloud (preferably to someone else) to check sense and punctuation.

Beware the word processing spell-checker

This tool will only pick up typographical errors and some grammatical errors: it will alert you to a misspelling of 'their', but won't always tell you if it should read 'there'.

Stick at it

You won't write your report all in one go, in one evening; it will take time and a number of drafts. Discipline yourself to write at a certain time of day or week, and use this time effectively. The best sort of writing is rewriting.

> **Study tip**
>
> Readers often read the introduction and conclusion of an academic report or essay first. This gives a feel for the overall shape and key arguments. Put effort into these parts and don't accept your first draft.

Structuring your report

When planning your report, it's important to think of the overall basic structure and the different elements you need to include. Consider the role that each of these elements will play.

Sections of your report

This table includes some of the sections you may wish to use in your report. Not all of these will be appropriate for your area of study although the introduction and conclusion must be included.

Section of the essay/report	What this means	Exemplar language
Abstract	A stand-alone, succinct summary of the main report/essay, laying out the purpose of the research, the methodology used, the key findings, and the main conclusion.	This report will compare and contrast… The question being discussed here… The argument puts forward…
Introduction	Explains the issue or problem which triggered the research and allows the reader to know what to expect by summarising its outline and structure.	To illustrate this finding… According to… The topic is limited by… Controversy has frequently arisen from…
Background research	This will highlight the breadth of your research, and make clear why these references are relevant to your own findings. It helps your reader understand the reasons or context for your study.	On the other hand … In contrast … Previous research on this topic uncovered… In 2011, the work carried out by XXX highlighted… There has been little recent interest in this topic, other than…
Conclusion	Summarises the research, 'answers' the main question, and draws together the main points of your argument.	To conclude … To sum up… Given this evidence… It can be seen that…
Discussion	An analysis and evaluation of the findings, and an evaluation of your own learning.	This justifies a fresh look at … In order to… On the other hand…
References	These include a note of the work of others that you have consulted during your research.	According to the work of XXX who asserted … (+ quote) XXX argues that … (+ paraphrase)
Evaluation of sources	Evidence of detailed research which involves the appropriate selection of sources which may be significant, unique, or provide an interesting perspective in the development of your findings.	XXX considered many perspectives… XXX denies… With this in mind… Significantly…
Bibliography	All the sources, printed and online, which you have consulted during your research, usually presented in alphabetical order. This allows the reader to go back to the original sources.	Tony Fry, 2017, Remaking cities – An Introduction to Urban Metrofitting: published by Bloomsbury Academic

3 Project management skills: producing the project product

> **ACTIVITY Structuring and writing your report**
>
> **1** Redraft the sentence on page 90 starting 'Keep sentences short…'. The redrafted sentences should be easier to read and understand.

> **Links**
>
> For more information on how to reference your sources and compile a bibliography, see pages 95–98.

What this means for my project

You need to select the most appropriate elements to include in your report, according to the style of your project and the subject matter. For most written research reports or investigations, the structure will be of standard academic format.

You need to include an introduction and a conclusion. What other elements you include will depend on the topic or field of your research. It is up to you to research the style used by professionals working in this field (for example scientists, historians, literature specialists). Look at what they do when they produce a research paper or report and make a decision as to what will best suit your subject area.

High marks go to students who address the question in the title directly, introducing referenced arguments and building up the debate, critically analysing the sources within the text and producing cross referenced supportive evidence or contradictory views. This builds up to a conclusion based securely on evidence and demonstrating judgment.

> **Study tip**
>
> You can prepare an abstract, but it is not a requirement to include one in your final report. The format of an academic abstract may be appropriate for you to include in your Production Log. It should be between 50–150 words long.

Avoid plagiarism

> **By the end of this section, you should be able to:**
> - ✔ explain the meaning of the word 'plagiarism'
> - ✔ identify pieces of writing that have been copied
> - ✔ understand how you can avoid plagiarism in your own Independent Project.

What is plagiarism?

Plagiarism is passing off somebody else's work as your own. It can range from getting someone else to write your work to simply cutting and pasting extracts from the Internet. It can also relate to not using references appropriately, and where you fail to acknowledge that an idea or argument comes from someone else's work.

At school you'd often describe this as 'cheating' or 'copying', and you know it's not right. **Copyright** law seeks to protect people's original work, making plagiarism illegal. Copyright laws may differ between countries but can cover plays, musical recordings and scores, literature, audio recordings, artistic works, broadcasts and films, and published works. The law allows authors to control the way their work is used. This means that any original piece of work cannot be copied or adapted unless the copyright owner agrees to it.

Coursework and project reports are often run through plagiarism-detection software by teachers and awarding bodies. Even rearranging the words, if you express someone else's idea you still need to acknowledge that the idea is theirs not yours.

It's not difficult to imagine how and why people plagiarise. Reasons could include:
- laziness – not making an effort to come up with another way of writing a phrase
- finding it difficult not to repeat phrases that a professional writer has used very well
- accidental – cutting and pasting notes from an article online, or copying notes without referencing them, so you believe it is your own work when you come to look at it later
- memorising – learning words by rote can lead to 'regurgitating' words without meaning to
- 'no one will notice' – it is blatant copyright infringement if you decide to take credit for someone else's hard work.

> **Study tip**
>
> Detailed reading and note-taking can result in plagiarism. Try to remember the main points in what you read rather than write out the actual words. Sometimes putting the information in a diagram such as a flow chart can help. You will need to sign the Candidate Record Form (CRF) to confirm that all work you submit is your own. You may be disqualified from the IPQ if you copy someone else's work, let someone copy your work, or cheat in any other way. Discuss this with your Supervisor if you are at all unsure.

3 Project management skills: producing the project product

ACTIVITY Plagiarism?

1 This extract is taken from the New Scientist article 'Controversial forensic DNA test gets the green light' (published 11 April 2008). Below are three ways of rephrasing the material. Work out which one would not be guilty of plagiarism.

> Although Caddy's report backs the science behind the analysis, it criticises the lack of uniformity in the way that police forensics teams collect and interpret DNA evidence, and the lack of awareness that contamination with DNA could falsify matches

A Even though Caddy's report backs the science behind the analysis, it doesn't back the lack of uniformity in the way that forensics teams collect and translate DNA evidence, and the fact they are not aware that contamination with DNA can falsify matches.

B Caddy has said that forensic teams do not all collect and interpret the evidence that they find. There is also the added problem of forensic teams not realising that contamination with other DNA can lead to the wrong conclusion.

C Caddy's report might have supported the analysis' science, but it criticises the lack of uniformity in the forensics team's collection and interpretation of DNA evidence, and that contamination with DNA could falsify matches.

2 Write down three ways in which you can avoid plagiarism in your own work. Consider how you take notes and make visuals from what you read. Which methods are less likely to result in the exact repetition of your sources?

What this means for my project

Your project requires you to develop your own ideas and arguments, and express them clearly. You need to discuss the work or opinions of others relevant to your project. To aim for a higher grade, you need to prove that you have selected sources 'for a clear and justified purpose' and that 'relevant information from them is identified systematically ad effectively. So take great care to use quotes or speech marks to show that someone's words are not your own. If you want to include a longer extract from a book or article, for example a whole paragraph, the convention is to indent the writing rather than using quotation marks. Use appropriate conventions for referencing your sources (see pages 95–98).

Key term

Plagiarism Copying someone else's work or recycling their ideas, and passing it off as your own either accidentally or through laziness.

Copyright Copyright usually belongs to the author of a piece of work (or sometimes the publisher) and prevents anyone else from reproducing their work.

: producing the project product

Referencing your sources

By the end of this section, you should be able to:
- ✔ understand the importance of referencing your sources
- ✔ appreciate there are accepted formats for referencing different types of sources
- ✔ understand how different referencing conventions are used in different subject areas.

Why do we need to reference sources?

There are a variety of accepted systems of referencing sources in academic work. These are usually based around broad subject disciplines, but they all do the same thing.

- Provide your reader with details about where they can go for more information.
- Present your work with authority, following best academic practice to assure readers that it is based on verifiable published research.
- Convince your reader that you have consulted a broad range of relevant published sources, topical or current in your field of research.
- Avoid plagiarism: by referencing other people's work you acknowledge that some ideas or phrases are not your own. (Even if you rework someone's words into your own, it is still a good academic practice to acknowledge the source of the ideas.)
- Support the evidence of your report, substantiating your arguments.

Referencing resources

Many schools and universities present their own guidelines for how they expect students to reference resources, such as the Harvard system of referencing. Professional societies or associations also have their own referencing conventions, as do the British Standards Institution. Follow the system used by academics writing in your subject area. You may have been taught some conventions which your teachers expect you to use.

Remember that for your Independent Project, the 5000 word limit does not include the bibliography.

Study tip
To create a bibliography/reference list for your Independent Project is an assessment requirement. If you don't provide one, your work cannot be graded. If you need any further help identifying the style of referencing you should use, discuss this with your Project Supervisor. Your Supervisor is there to support you.

3 Project management skills: producing the project product

How should you reference?
Remember there are two parts to referencing:
1. Identify another's work in the main body of your text to give a brief outline of the published work.
2. Record your sources in a bibliography or in a reference list at the end of your report.

There are also different types of sources that you need to refer to – it's not just books and journals. These may have their own styles of referencing which is important to follow.

ACTIVITY Sources to reference

1. Think of as many different types of source as you can – ones you might want to reference in your report.

Print	Electronic	Audio	Visual	Other
Published music score	Email	Recorded music	Film	

2. Consider websites.

   A What types of websites are likely to be most suitable for you to reference in your project?

   B Are any types of website less suitable for referencing in an academic context?

Study tip You are encouraged to use professional and academic sources for your project and not to rely too heavily on 'superficial' internet sites or social media. Remember: evaluate all sources in the same way to validate their authority.

Top tips for accurate referencing
- When you do your research, note the style of referencing used in the books and journals you consult. This provides good guidance on referencing in your subject area.
- Keep a sheet of notes of all your sources from the day you start your research. This will help you to keep an accurate record, and it will also save you time should you need to go back to one of your sources.
- Once you've decided to follow a particular style of referencing, be consistent in how you apply it. It won't look good to mix and match the different conventions.

Key term

Referencing Listing the full and original source so that readers might find it.

Citation When you quote or highlight a source in the main body of your text. If you cite a text, you point out to readers that the text or idea is not your own.

- Most of the information you require for referencing printed materials, particularly books, will be found on the title page or on the reverse of the title page.
- If you are in any doubt as to whether you should reference a source, it probably represents better practice to include it.

If you are using a direct quotation, make sure to reproduce it accurately word for word.

Main referencing systems

Modern Language Association of America (MLA)

In literary subject areas, the MLA system of referencing is often adopted. It is an economical approach to referencing, providing the reader with the least they need to know. For books:

Highlight references in the main body of your text. Your text flags another person's ideas (+ original author's family name + page reference), for example: "One well-known researcher criticised Austen for her detailed portrayal (Harrison 221)".

Then list the full information in your bibliography/reference list.

Author's family name + given name + Title + place of publication + publisher + date of publication, for example: Harrison, James. *The World of Clementine Austen*. Cheltenham. Nelson Thornes Publishers. 2009.

To cite other sources, such as journals, online journals, personal communication, or newspaper articles, you will need to research precise guidelines from the MLA.

American Psychological Association/British Psychological Society (APA/BPS)

Very similar *to* the Harvard referencing system, these recommendations are relevant for psychology, health sciences, and nursing subject areas. For a full guide to the APA system, consult the *Publication Manual of the American Psychological Association*. For books: Highlight references in the main body of your text.

An author plus date of publication system is used. For example: "In a recent study, Brown (2006) found that there was …"

OR

"Beliefs in our own culture are often undermined by …" (Smith, 1967)

Then list the full information in your bibliography/reference list.

Author's family name + initial + *Title* + place of publication + publisher + date of publication. For example:

"Smith, T. *Psychology in Our Times*. Cheltenham. Nelson Thornes Publishers. 1967."

3 Project management skills: producing the project product

Chicago Manual of Style documentation system (CMS)

A scheme used for citing humanities/socials sciences subject areas. For books:

Highlight references in the main body of your text.

The CMS referencing system follows similar rules to the APA and emphasises the author and date of publication when citing in the main body of text.

Then list the full information in your bibliography/reference list.

Although the first line of an entry is left-justified on your page, second and third lines are indented by five spaces. Arranged alphabetically, entries are:

Author's family name + (usually) initial + title/subtitle in initial capital only

ACTIVITY Referencing systems

You will need to decide on the appropriate referencing system for your subject area. Research how this system advises you to cite the following types of documents:

Documentation	In-text citation style	Reference listing style
Books		
Journals		
Websites		
Newspaper articles		
Personal correspondence		

Remember that you will have to understand both stages of the process:

how to cite the work in the main body of your text

how to list the full information in your reference list/bibliography

Study tip

When referencing and quoting other works, try to avoid writing anything you don't understand. Don't be tempted to include something just 'because it sounds good'. You need to be in control of your own writing. This might mean leaving some ideas out as much as including others.

Key term

Bibliography A listing of all the books, documents and online resources you consulted throughout your research.

Reference list A list at the end of your report which provides readers with more information on the sources cited in your work.

3 Project management skills: producing the project product

Oxford AQA Exams IPQ Assessment Objectives[1]

Now is a good time to remind yourself of the Oxford International AQA Exams Assessment Objectives for your Independent Project, and check that you are on track to achieve the best grade possible for your hard work. Use the Candidate Record Form, Production Log & Assessment Record to record this process. Your written report is the 'product' of all your research and hard work. The Oxford AQA Exams IPQ spec regularly refers to the report you write at the end of your research as a 'project product'.

The next stage of your research will be to meet with your Supervisor for your project product review meeting. It is worth preparing for that discussion by reviewing the criteria by which your project product (or report) will be assessed.

The relevant Assessment Objectives at this stage are listed below:

Assessment Objective	Grading Criteria
AO3 **Demonstration of research skills** • Research a range of resources? • Examine the resources critically • Organise the information and resources you gather • Justify the selection of any secondary and primary resources you use	**Grade A** 'Sources are selected for a clear and justified purpose and relevant information from them is identified systematically and effectively. Sources are subjected to scrutiny to assess their validity.' *In other words:* To achieve a high grade, you need to make sure your resources are relevant and describe how you have assessed that they are valid evidence in your written report. If your justification for selecting certain resources is inconsistent, or you have not always shown how you examined and scrutinised your sources for their validity and appropriateness, then you may achieve a lower grade.
AO4 **Analysis and application of research** • Implement the project plan • Analyse the findings of the project research • Arrange these findings in a 5000 word report • Include a conclusion to your report and communicate your outcomes • Include a bibliography and references and any other appropriate appendices to your report	**Grade A** 'The report is of appropriate length and writing style, with a clear focus on the final title throughout. The project is organised well and referenced appropriately.' *In other words:* To be awarded a higher grade, you need to do an accurate word count to ensure your writing is within the 5000 word limit (+/- 10%). Remember your bibliography/reference list or any description of sources or any reasons you have for selecting the sources is *not* included in this word count. 'Selected information and/or sources are synthesized into a compelling report that leads to a well evidenced conclusion.' *In other words:* To be awarded a higher grade, your project report will communicate your findings clearly and your discussion will be robust and persuasive. Your conclusion logically leads from a set of well-balanced evidence and your writing suggests a strong subject knowledge. If your report is disorganised, lacks focus, and you have, for example, included a conclusion, but there are gaps in your evidence, and it is not always clear and appropriate, then you will achieve one of the lower grades.

---

[1] © Oxford International AQA Exams Please refer to the current version of the specification on the Oxford AQA Exams website at www.oxfordaqaexams.org.uk/subjects/projects/ipq

3 Project management skills: producing the project product

Assessment Objective	Grading Criteria
AO5 **Evaluation of product, process and self** • Evaluate the strengths and weaknesses of the project process and your report • Review your own learning through the entire project	Grade A 'There is detailed and insightful evaluation of the strengths and weaknesses of both the final report and the organisation of the project. The student reflects on his/her own learning in a detailed and insightful manner.'
	In other words: To be awarded a higher grade, you must offer detailed evaluation of both the project process (eg how you organised and monitored your project) and give consideration to the strengths and weaknesses of the final report. You should offer a detailed evaluation of your own learning providing insight into how you learned, what you learned, and how your project research evolved as a result of your learning. Above all, you must ensure your writing is evaluative and critical. The more descriptive your writing, the more likely you will be awarded a lower grade (or your work is ungraded).
(This highlights the most relevant aspects of the Assessment Objective at this stage in your project; for a full account of all AOs, see page 40)	

3 Project management skills: producing the project product

List of required material for grading[2]

Before your work can be given a grade, you must ensure that you have produced (and provided evidence for) each of the following:

	Required material for assessment	What you provide/where you provide the evidence
1	You have selected an area of interest for your project research	• Candidate Record Form, Production Log and Assessment Record
2	You have set a working title for your project	• Candidate Record Form, Production Log and Assessment Record
3	You have undertaken a risk assessment	• Candidate Record Form, Production Log and Assessment Record • Additional planning evidence may be presented in an appendix
4	You have produced a project plan	• If appropriate, as an appendix to your Candidate Record Form, Production Log and Assessment Record
5	You have implemented your project plan and documented any changes you made to it	• Candidate Record Form, Production Log and Assessment Record
6	You have produced a written report addressing your final title of 5000 words in length (+/− 10%)	• Your written report
7	You used a referencing method in your research report	• Your written report
8	You communicated your findings in the report and in a live presentation	• Your written report • Evidence of a presentation is provided in the Production Log
9	You created a bibliography/reference list	• As an appendix to your written report
10	You evaluated the strengths and weaknesses of the project	• Candidate Record Form, Production Log, and Assessment Record
	Before submission, a signed and completed Candidate Record Form, Production Log, and Assessment Record must be provided	• All pages of the Candidate Record Form, Production Log, and Assessment Record are completed

Key term

Authentication (of work) All the work for your IPQ must be your own. You are asked to confirm that the work you submit is original and carried out by you, by signing the Candidate Record Form. Your Project Supervisor must also sign the declaration of authentication on this form, to confirm that they believe the project is authentic, original and your own work.

Malpractice This refers to improper or illegal behaviour. In an academic context, it refers to bad practice where, for example, you might submit work that you copied from someone else's project, or that you asked someone else to type up for you, but you have not acknowledged their work. Plagiarism is a form of malpractice.

---

[2]© Oxford International AQA Exams Please refer to the current version of the specification on the Oxford AQA Exams website at www.oxfordaqaexams.org.uk/subjects/projects/ipq

3 Project management skills: producing the project product

Checklist – are you ready for your project product review meeting?

As part of the assessment evidence for your Extended Project, you are required to discuss your project with your Supervisor at a project product review meeting. This stage is important in the journey of your International IPQ. It allows you to review your work, highlight successes and failures, and help you to make any changes or additions to help you achieve a better grade. Your Supervisor will be very willing to discuss this review process, and to support you in completing your Oxford AQA Exams Candidate Record form, Production Log & Assessment Record.

Use this checklist to make sure you're appropriately prepared.[3]

The best style of presentation for my report is …	
The different features I will use in my report are …	
The audience for my report can be described as …	
The best way to communicate my findings and ideas to my audience is …	
I will make sure I use the most appropriate language and terminology by …	
I will avoid plagiarism by …	
The planned sections of my report are ……….	
The planned word count for each section is ………	
I have backed up my findings by ……….	
The most appropriate referencing system for my report is …………	
The questions I want to ask my Supervisor at my project product review meeting are:	
What else do I need to do? By when? (give date)	

---

[3] Filling in this chart is not an AQA requirement for your IPQ. However it may help you to prepare for a meeting with your Supervisor.

3 Project management skills: producing the project product

Producing your project product

▶ **1 Project management skills: starting out**

▶ **2 Project management skills: researching the project**

▼ **3 Project management skills: producing the project product**

Have you discussed your project at a project product review meeting?	Yes No
Have you completed page 14 of your Project Production Log & Assessment Record?	Yes No
Have you considered and finalised the format for your report and appropriate appendices?	Yes No

▶ **4 Presenting your project**

▶ **5 Finalising and submitting your project**

▶▶▶ Next steps

The next stage of your Independent Project Qualification will be to plan and deliver the ten-minute live presentation of your project. This would usually take the form of a verbal presentation, and it may involve the use of slides, PowerPoint, or short excerpts of video material. You will also be required to answer questions in a live 10-minute Q and A session, as a follow-up to your presentation.

▶▶▶

4 Presenting your project

It takes a great deal of courage to present your own work to an audience. Whatever form you decide on for your project presentation, good preparation will help you to relax and enjoy the experience. You should aim to present your work and the evidence of what you've learned in the most effective and interesting way for your audience. Your project may explore complex ideas in a specialist area. In your presentation you have to make these understandable to an audience for whom these may be new concepts.

This chapter will help you to:
- ✔ identify the best style of presentation for your project
- ✔ explore the structure of your presentation
- ✔ understand the pros and cons of presentation software
- ✔ communicate your message clearly and appropriately for your audience
- ✔ prepare and deliver a ten-minute live presentation
- ✔ overcome nerves and respond confidently to questions after your presentation.

Some people are natural communicators, but most people can improve with practice.

Different presentation styles: what should your presentation consist of?

> **By the end of this section, you should be able to:**
> - ✔ identify good and bad practice in the delivery of a presentation
> - ✔ explore which form your own presentation might take
> - ✔ understand the objectives of your presentation and decide what it is best to include – and leave out of – your presentation

Different styles of presentation

Your presentation is a compulsory part of the IPQ and should take the form of a verbal presentation. It should last ten minutes. You can use presentation software if you like, but you do not have to. You should assume that you are speaking to a non-specialist audience.

Oxford AQA Exams specify that the the minimum number of people in the audience is two (one of these should be your Project Supervisor).

However, each school will have their own arrangements for students' IPQ presentations, so it is important you discuss this with your Supervisor and understand how your school would like you to deliver it. Your audience may turn out to be bigger than this.

You can deliver the presentation in English or in your own home language. If you don't deliver your presentation in English, then an authenticated translation must be provided. All written evidence, including any slides or posters you include, must be provided in English.

To help you decide on the form your presentation will take, it's worth considering good and bad practice and thinking about your own strengths and weaknesses. Would a short verbal presentation best represent you and your project work, for example?

What this means for my project

Identify the characteristics of your audience before you start writing. You need to imagine each member of the audience as an educated non-specialist with little prior knowledge of the subject. Imagine they have a good general knowledge, so they can interpret challenging material if it is clearly expressed and appropriately communicated.

ACTIVITY Thinking about presentations

1 Think about some presentations where you have been part of the audience. Note down:
- characteristics of talks you have enjoyed (good practice)
- characteristics of talks that have bored you (bad practice).

2 Think about your own strengths and weaknesses. Give yourself marks out of ten for each of these statements, depending on how closely you believe they match you.

	1-6 marks	7 marks or more
I rarely suffer nerves when talking about something that really interests me		
I love getting up in front of an audience and am used to taking the stage		
I enjoy being challenged by unexpected questions		
I'm never intimidated by an audience, whether of 2 or 102 people!		
If I prepare well and schedule my timings carefully, I usually do well		

What should your presentation include?

You need to balance what you want to say with what your audience wants to hear. People like to hear an enthusiast talk about what interests them, but be aware of what will interest your particular audience. Your presentation has to suit a non-specialist audience. Avoid jargon unless you understand and can fully explain this level of technical vocabulary.

Think about the structure of your presentation

Structure your presentation so that it has three main sections:

1. **Introduction:** or 'Tell your audience what you are going to tell them.' Let them know how long it will take, say briefly what you will talk about in each section of the presentation, and say why you are the best person to present this topic.
2. **The main section:** 'Tell them.' This should cover both the content and process of your project.
3. **Conclusion:** 'Tell them what you've told them.' Sum up your key messages.

Think about the venue

Where you deliver your presentation will affect the content and form it should take. Think about:
- What resources are available? Is there a projector or video screen you can use, for example?
- Are there any constraints in terms of space, lighting, audience size, and so on

4 Presenting your project

What this means for my project

Discuss the best style of presentation for your project with your Supervisor. Talk about what resources you need to prepare to match the content of your project, what you want to say, and the resources you have available. You also need to be ready to answer questions.

During the presentation you will be assessed by your Supervisor. Your Supervisor will ask questions that:

explore your understanding of the project's material – its **content**

explore the **process** of your project, and ask why you made particular choices during your research and production work.

Study tip

For assessment purposes, you need to demonstrate what you have learned.

Just using long words will not convince your audience that you know what you are talking about. It is better to use everyday language and avoid jargon. Better still, use the necessary technical language, carefully explaining what it means. You have to be a real expert to be able to explain complex ideas at a simple level. You could use metaphors or carefully chosen diagrams to 'teach' your audience and demonstrate your expertise. ('Breaking the ice' when you get to know someone is an example of a metaphor.) If English is not your home language, but you will deliver your presentation in English, then this tip is valid for you as well. If English is not your home language, but you will deliver your presentation in English, then this tip is valid for you as well.

Presentation skills

> **By the end of this section, you should be able to:**
> - identify the pros and cons of using presentation software
> - make use of some techniques for getting your message across effectively
> - manage your nerves during the presentation
> - rehearse your presentation, including preparing for questions.

Using presentation software

Probably the worst way to start with planning your presentation is by starting to put together a set of electronic slides. Your presentation software is produced for the benefit of your audience, not for you, the presenter. It is not a presentation in itself but a support or visual aid to enhance your presentation.

It's probably best to plan the structure and content of your presentation before you put the slides together. The slides then form a back up or reinforcement of your message rather than driving what you say.

ACTIVITY Using presentation software: pros and cons

Think about the pros and cons of using a software presentation package. Consider:

A   the presenter's needs

B   the audience's experience

C   how the presentation software might affect the delivery of the message

	Pros	Cons
a)		
b)		
c)		

4 Presenting your project

Golden rules for presentation slides to impress your audience

- Keep flying objects, sound effects, choice of colours, and animations to a minimum: avoid visual chaos.
- Create the right number of slides for the time you have available (roughly one per minute).
- Carefully edit and proof read your slides (before your audience does).
- Use the same font size throughout. Check you can read it at the distance of your audience. Keep text to a minimum. The words are just a short prompt for you.
- Only use capital letters for emphasis or impact: they imply that you're SHOUTING at your audience.
- Provide hand-outs for sections of text your audience needs to read, or for complex diagrams and data which will not come across effectively on slides.

ACTIVITY Props and visual aids

1. What other items might you use as a prop or visual aid to emphasise a point? Think of examples of each of:
   - something for your audience to taste
   - something for your audience to listen to
   - something for your audience to touch
   - something for your audience to try out
   - a moving image or video clip for your audience to watch.

ACTIVITY Assessing visual aids

1. Think about these questions in relation to your own slide presentation and visual aids.
   - A Does each slide or visual aid add a useful and important message?
   - B Will everyone, including those at the back of the room, be able to read all the slides and see the visual aids?
   - C Are there any slides where a picture, diagram or photo enhances your message better than text?
   - D Is each slide clear and simple: no more than six lines of text?
2. Switch off your computer and sketch out one slide for each main section of your presentation. These are probably the only slides that you'll need. Look again and reassure yourself that each slide needs to be there.

Communicating clearly

Clear communication is made up of several factors. You engage your audience through your personality and though your interaction with them, as well as through what you have to say.

No doubt, nerves are going to play their part. However, always remember that the audience or panel for your IPQ presentation will be sympathetic and keen that you do well. They're on your side!

Tips for presenting in English (even when English is not your home language)

It can feel intimidating for anyone to speak in front of a group of people, but if you feel your English is not as proficient as some other students, you might take note of these tips to give you some confidence:

1. **Practise the pronunciation** of technical language, or language that you use less frequently with a teacher/someone whose first language is English. But try and avoid jargon. Use plain English – your audience will thank you for it.
2. **Speak slowly** – we all have our own personal accent, so to help your audience adapt to *your* accent, talk slowly and speak up. Talking slowly is important for all presenters. In fact, your speech is probably slow enough, once it feels strange to you. Slowing down will also help you avoid introducing redundant language and saying things that perhaps don't need to be said.
3. **Work out a 'crisis' strategy**. If you have trouble understanding a question that is asked of you at the end of your session, look at a native English speaker (a teacher or a friend) and say 'Could you help me understand the question?'. And if you should forget a key word or how to say something in English – what should you do? Ask your audience! It helps build a relationship and your audience will always want you to do well.
4. **Learn how to use key transition phrases**. Help your audience to understand the flow of your presentation, and how your argument is connected by using transition words, such as:
   - First
   - Meanwhile
   - On the other hand
   - In this case
   - Evidence of this
   - In addition
   - It's important to realise that
   - As illustration
   - In spite of
   - With this in mind
   - In other words
   - To sum up
   - In conclusion
   - As you can see

5. **Write notes on small cards to prepare for your presentation**. Writing out a full script for what you need to say won't work. It won't sound natural. But brief notes to help you with the key items you need to say (and any important data or quotes, for example), will help you sound natural – and will also help with your nerves.
6. **Practise, practise, practise**. Practise with your notes in front of the mirror. It will help build your confidence if you've already heard yourself speak a number of times, and proved to yourself that you can do it!

Above all, if you focus on the content of your presentation, rather than how it's said, this will make the presentation easier. No one is better qualified to deliver your presentation than you! If you know your information well, have done some thorough research, are familiar with the data you gathered and what you have learned from it, then this will give you confidence.

Using body language effectively

When you are talking to someone, research suggests that the meaning of what you are saying is conveyed via the words you use, the tone of your voice and your body language – in the following proportions:

- 55% body language
- 38% the tone of your voice
- 7% the words you use.

Surprising, isn't it? But we all know that feelings show on people's faces even before we hear what they are saying.

This doesn't necessarily mean that you should fake or develop your body language, but simply to be more aware of it and use it to your advantage. Positive posture can add impact to what you are saying.

A friend could film you on their phone so you can watch yourself critically!

> **Study tip**
>
> The old cliché that a picture tells a thousand words may be true. Sometimes it's more effective to think in terms of what a slide shows rather than what it says. Remember that the media or format of your presentation must be entirely in line with the type of project.

> **Key term**
>
> **Body language** Our subconscious mannerisms, facial expressions, hand gestures, eye contact, and all those aspects of non-verbal communication which enhance (or possibly detract from) a message.

4 Presenting your project

ACTIVITY Body language

Consider these examples of body language and behaviour. Discuss which you think would be most effective in your own presentation:

1A You enter a room to listen to a presentation. The speaker has arrived, and is standing ready at the front of the room.

or

1B Sitting in the audience you are waiting for the speaker. He arrives, rushing into the room, looking for a socket to plug his laptop into.

2A A presenter stands with a folder held tightly in front of them while speaking.

or

2B A presenter stands facing the audience with their feet slightly apart, arms moving naturally.

3A A presenter gesticulates with their hands and arms in a way which emphasises their enthusiasm.

or

3B A presenter repeatedly fiddles with their hair and clothing.

4A A presenter looks down at the floor while speaking.

or

4B A presenter maintains eye contact with different members of the audience.

Positive posture might include:
- ✔ Facing the audience when you are describing the content of a slide, rather than turning to face the slide
- ✔ Standing with shoulders back and head up rather than hunching over your notes
- ✔ Thinking 'tall' (imagine someone is pulling a thread attached to the top of your head) – this automatically helps you adopt a more confident posture
- ✔ Arriving before your audience, so that you 'own' the space
- ✔ Standing in front of a desk or table to make you appear more confident. Behind it, you'll look more nervous and defensive.

Dealing with nerves

How do you feel about presenting your project? Nervous? Research has shown that the number one fear for most adults is public speaking. Even the most experienced presenters have to focus on overcoming their nerves before getting up in front of an audience or panel.

More often than not, we appear more nervous to ourselves than to our audience. Presentation nerves are usually driven by a fear of what might go wrong. So, once you get started, if you have planned well and practised your presentation, you know your equipment is working and your audience look interested, the nerves often subside.

ACTIVITY Dealing with nerves

1. When was the last time you felt nervous?
   - How does it affect how you speak? Do you speak more quickly or more slowly?
   - Does your mouth run away with you so that you speak before you think?
   - Do you giggle or appear more sullen?
   - Do you pretend you don't suffer from nerves at all, and come across as 'not really you' or maybe a bit arrogant?
2. Have you tried out any techniques to manage these nerves? Ask your friends or teachers how they manage nerves.

Once you've decided on what you're going to say, and your slides and visual aids are prepared, you need to rehearse your presentation. This will help you to feel comfortable with your subject and with your timings.

A rehearsal stage will help you to:
- ✔ Talk through your presentation rather than read your notes.
- ✔ Start by typing your presentation as if you were going to read it.
- ✔ Use a large font and double line spacing to keep it clear.
- ✔ Read it through a few times silently.
- ✔ Then read it aloud.
- ✔ Read it aloud while standing up – possibly in front of a mirror.
- ✔ Read through it and practise the sort of arm movements or facial expressions you would normally use

This rehearsal process will help you remember much of what you need to say and make it sound entirely natural. Familiarity brings confidence. Your notes will then be a useful prompt only if you need them.

- Familiarise yourself with the venue and with any equipment such as a data projector, to help you feel more 'at home'.
- Time your presentation and keep to schedule. When you are planning your presentation, allocate a number of minutes to each section. When practising, check your timings against a watch. During your presentation, place a clock or watch where you can see it without looking down at your wrist.
- Discuss your presentation with your Supervisor. They will be able to advise you on how to prepare.

Memory tips

If you have 'learned' your presentation, so that you can remember the pain points, this will help you to feel more confident and relaxed. Don't memorise it word-for-word, but it is important to have a way of remembering the sequence of ideas you will present.

Use **prompt cards** rather than full notes, so the key themes and ideas are summarised and you can remind yourself at a glance.

Use a **memory strategy** such as mnemonics or 'use of loci (places)' to help order your ideas. Use an online search engine to find out more about these.

> **ACTIVITY Researching memory techniques**
>
> Research a memory technique which is useful for remembering lists of items or ideas. Explain this technique to two other students, and listen to the ideas they have researched.

Preparing for questions

Your Supervisor will be required to ask questions about your presentation. They will be looking to:
- explore your understanding of the topic
- understand the choices you made in your research and the development of your project.

Examples of the type of question you may be asked
- Tell me about how you arrived at this topic choice.
- Why is your topic important?
- Describe one of the problems you faced, and how you arrived at a solution.
- Outline any additions or changes you made as a result of one of your review meetings.
- If you had to advise someone on doing a project like yours, what one piece of advice would you give?
- Could you explain exactly what you mean by 'XXX'?
- There may also be some questions specific to your project, perhaps asking you to expand on or explain some of your research findings.

What should you do if you get a difficult question? Allow yourself space to think about your answer rather than responding too quickly. Don't try and pretend you know the answer when you know you don't. If you really don't know, say so, and suggest ways that you could find out the answer.

4 Presenting your project

Checklist – are you ready for your presentation and question and answer session?

As part of the assessment evidence for your Independent Project, you are required to present your project work to your Supervisor (and others). You need to prepare well and to bear in mind who your presentation is for. You want to present your work in the best light, so that you can demonstrate exactly what you've learned, and provide evidence of the skills you've developed.

You may also seek advice from your Supervisor in advance of the presentation itself. This, in turn, will support you in completing page 15 of your Oxford AQA Exams Candidate Record form, Production Log & Assessment Record.

Use this checklist to make sure you're appropriately prepared.[1]

	Comments on your next steps	
I have discussed ideas for my presentation with my Supervisor, and the form it will take is …		
The points of good and bad practice I have considered are …	Good practice	Bad practice
PowerPoint will/ will not be an appropriate software package for me to use because …		
The skills I will draw on to create my slide presentation are …		
I am confident enough in my subject matter to answer questions about my report findings. Questions I could be asked include …		

---

[1] Filling in this chart is not an Oxford AQA Exams requirement for your IPQ. However, it may help you prepare for a meeting with your Supervisor.

4 Presenting your project

	Comments on your next steps		
The main points about the content and process of my project which I will cover in my presentation are …	Content		Process
I've rehearsed my presentation either in front of the mirror or in front of an audience, and my reflections on the practice presentation are …	Good points		Points I could improve
I've timed my presentation and it takes …	……………….. minutes		
The features of my body language that I could improve on are …			
The particular needs, areas of interest and level of prior knowledge of my audience are …			
I've had a look at the venue for my presentation, and the points to note are …			
What else do I need to do?			

Project progress checkpoint

▶ **1** Project management skills: starting out

▶ **2** Project management skills: researching the project

▶ **3** Project management skills: producing the project product

▼ **4** Presenting your project

Have you discussed your presentation with your Supervisor?	Yes	No
Have you given your presentation?	Yes	No
Have you completed page 15 of your Oxford AQA Exams Candidate Record Form, Production Log & Assessment Record?	Yes	No

▶ **5** Finalising and submitting your project

▶▶▶ **Next steps**

The next stage of your Independent Project Qualification is to finalise your project. This will involve an evaluation of your work which will then lead to your final submission ▶▶▶

Finalising and submitting your project | 5

With much of the hard work on your project and presentation completed, there is still one last step. You need to understand the processes of evaluation and reflection, and apply the principles to your own learning.

Reflection is a requirement for IPQ assessment purposes: you must 'evaluate the strengths and weaknesses of the project process (including review of own learning arising from it) and product', as outlined in the Assessment Objective AO5 against which your work will be judged. At the same time, this evaluation and reflection process helps you to learn from the independent project process you have carried out. Independent learning is all about taking responsibility. It's up to you to reflect on what went well, and where you could do better. This allows you to build on the skills you may need in the future, and apply these in a range of situations.

> **This chapter will help you to:**
> ✔ identify the criteria for evaluation, and define what we mean by reflection
> ✔ practise the processes of evaluation and reflection
> ✔ complete page 18 of your IPQ Candidate Record Form, Production Log & Assessment Record.

Keeping to a word limit is an important discipline to learn.

5 Finalising and submitting your project

Evaluation and reflection

By the end of this section, you should be able to:
- ✔ carry out evaluation and reflection on the learning process and content of your project
- ✔ use evaluation and reflection as part of your learning process.

In order to evaluate your learning of the topic and processes involved in your project, you first need to consider the stages you have carried out:
- choosing a topic
- researching your topic, including the resources you used and those you chose not to use; how you made use of technology and any other tools; the decision making, problem solving and critical thinking processes you were able to draw on
- writing your report
- presenting your project.

When you evaluate these stages, you need to consider:
- what you learned about the topic
- pros and cons of the processes you used
- strengths and weaknesses of various techniques
- what went well and what didn't go so well.

Your reflections and evaluation will help you to learn from your experiences and approach similar tasks more effectively in the future.

> **Key term**
>
> **Evaluation** to weigh up the good points and bad points of the content and learning process associated with your project with reference to the criteria for success
>
> **Reflection** to give something serious thought and consideration

5 Finalising and submitting your project

What this means for my project

Your Oxford AQA Independent Project work will be judged against a set of Assessment Objectives and Grading Criteria including:

- AO5: Evaluation of product, process and self
  Evaluate the strengths and weaknesses of the project process (including review of own learning from it) and product.

ACTIVITY Reviewing your work

1. Go back through your Production Log and consider each stage of your project work. Consider these questions.
   - **What** skills have you learned?
   - **How** might you use these skills in the future, or in other areas of study?
   - **What** did you particularly enjoy about learning this topic?
   - **Were** there elements of this topic that you found less interesting?
   - **How** well do you think you carried out the research, applied the research to your project, and wrote and carried out your presentation? What went particularly well?
   - **What** could you have done better?
   - **What** would you do differently if you were to do this project again?
   - **What** piece of advice would you give a friend if they were going to do a similar project?
   - **How** well did you achieve the aims you identified at the planning stage?

5 Finalising and submitting your project

Completing your Project Production Log

By the end of this section, you should be able to:
- ✔ Explore some of the language you might use in the process of evaluation.
- ✔ Complete page 18 of your Oxford AQA Exams Candidate Record Form, Production Log & Assessment Record.

To complete page 18 of your Oxford AQA Exams Candidate Record Form, Project Production Log & Assessment Record, you need to discuss your learning and the processes involved in your project work. You should combine this with your judgement of your performance on these aspects of your project. You will need to:

- Provide evidence to support your judgements and conclusions
- Communicate your logic very clearly, using appropriate language
- Keep it relevant: only include information which you can back up with evidence.

5 Finalising and submitting your project

ACTIVITY Evaluating and reporting on your own work

1. Talk to another student who is also producing an Independent Project. Discuss your reflections and thoughts on evaluating your project. Sometimes hearing someone else's ideas helps trigger a fresh way of looking at your own work.

2. Consider the language you include in your Production Log.

   A Think about the **language of conclusions**, for example: what this means is …, it is possible to conclude that …, evidence shows that …, it is clear that… What other ideas do you have?

   Think about the **language of judgement**. You may use a direct statement, such as 'this was fascinating' or 'this evidence was not backed up by other research'. You may use nouns such as 'In my view, …' or 'In my opinion, …'. You could compare and contrast the opinions of others that you have researched. What else?

   B When might it be appropriate to use 'must' or 'should'. For example: 'the next stage must be …' or 'the team should look into the impact of their exhibition on …'

Study tip Remember that just because you feel or believe something does not put it beyond question. In your report you need to be able to provide evidence of your opinion and back up your conclusions.

Links

Go to page 71 for more information on creative thinking, and how to encourage yourself to think about an issue with a fresh eye.

5 Finalising and submitting your project

Checklist – are you ready for your project submission?

As part of the assessment evidence for your Independent Project at this stage in your work, you are required to:
- complete the Oxford AQA Exams Candidate Record Form, Production Log & Assessment Record
- sign the declaration on this form to confirm that the work is your own (other than where you have acknowledged the sources of information you have used, and the expected support that you have received)
- submit your final work.

Use this checklist to make sure you're appropriately prepared.[1]

	Comment on your next steps	
The main points that I have learned about my project's topic are…		
What I enjoyed about studying this topic is…		
The aspects I thought were less interesting about this topic are…		
The skills I have developed through this project are…		
The skills I will use in the future, and the ways I will use these are…		
The areas of my project that went really well are…		
The areas of my performance that I could improve in the future are…		
If I were to do this project again, the things I would do differently (and the reasons for these changes) are…		
The advice I would give a friend if they were going to start on a project like this is…		
My final proof reading of my report for inaccuracies and errors was important because…		
The sort of changes I made in the quality of language in my report included…		
I have completed page 18 of the Oxford AQA Exams Candidate Record Form, Production Log & Assessment Report	Yes	No
What else do I need to do?…		

---

[1] Filling in this chart is not an Oxford AQA Exams requirement for IPQ. However it may help you to prepare for a meeting with your supervisor.

Project progress checkpoint

▶ 1 Project management skills: starting out

▶ 2 Project management skills: researching the project

▶ 3 Project management skills: producing the project product

▶ 4 Presenting your project

▼ 5 Finalising and submitting your project

Have you discussed the submission of your Project with your Supervisor?	Yes	No
Have you checked your report?	Yes	No
Have you completed page 18 of your Oxford AQA Exams Candidate Record Form, Production Log & Assessment Record?	Yes	No

Notes

Notes

Notes